9

Article on G. M. Hopkins —
with pictures — in
Jubilee, May, 1955, p. 20.

GERARD MANLEY HOPKINS

THE MAKERS OF
MODERN LITERATURE SERIES

"*James Joyce*" by Harry Levin
"*Virginia Woolf*" by David Daiches
"*E M Forster*" by Lionel Trilling
"*Nikolai Gogol*" by Vladimir Nabokov
"*Garcia Lorca*" by Edwin Honig
"*Gerard Manley Hopkins*" by The Kenyon Critics
"*T S Eliot*" by Delmore Schwartz
"*Edwin Arlington Robinson*" by Yvor Winters

others in preparation

GERARD MANLEY HOPKINS
1880

Gerard Manley Hopkins

BY THE KENYON CRITICS

THE MAKERS OF MODERN LITERATURE

New Directions Books - Norfolk, Connecticut

THE MAKERS OF MODERN LITERATURE SERIES

James Joyce by Harry Levin

Virginia Woolf by David Daiches

E. M. Forster by Lionel Trilling

García Lorca by Edwin Honig

Nikolai Gogol by Vladimir Nabokov

G. M. Hopkins by The Kenyon Critics

Others in preparation

MANUFACTURED IN THE UNITED STATES
BY THE VAIL-BALLOU PRESS

*New Directions Books Are Published by
James Laughlin*

NEW YORK OFFICE—500 FIFTH AVENUE

14186

THE KENYON CRITICS

Robert Lowell - Herbert Marshall McLuhan
F. R. Leavis - Josephine Miles - Arthur Mizener
Harold Whitehall - Austin Warren

WITH THE EXCEPTION OF MR. LEAVIS' ESSAY, WHICH FIRST appeared in *Scrutiny,* and Mr. Warren's biographical chapter, the component parts of the book were first published in the pages of *The Kenyon Review,* which marked the centennial anniversary of Hopkins' birth by inviting a group of critics to examine various aspects of his work. To the editor of the *Review,* Mr. John Crowe Ransom, who initiated the project, and to the guest editor, Mr. Cleanth Brooks, Jr., who carried it through, the publisher expresses the gratitude which admirers of Hopkins will feel for this book.

A C K N O W L E D G M E N T

QUOTATIONS FROM THE WORK OF HOPKINS IN THIS BOOK ARE taken from the authorized texts, which are published by The Oxford University Press, New York.

CONTENTS

1. GERARD MANLEY HOPKINS
   (1844–1889)

By Austin Warren

THE ITINERARY OF GERARD MANLEY HOPKINS' LIFE IS A LIST
of schools, universities, seminaries, and parish churches.
The crisis of his life lay, without doubt, in the passage
from Anglicanism to Catholicism and the adjacent deci-
sions to become a priest and a Jesuit. To the literary world,
there is drama, certainly, in his seven-years renunciation
of writing poetry, made upon his joining the Jesuits.—But
the high pitch of his temperament made all his days
abound in momentous decisions and crises. His conscience
was as trigger-poised as his sensibility.

From childhood on, his pattern seems consistent. He is
an aesthete and an ascetic,—always more or less, and in-
creasingly, aware that the latter must curb and stiffen
and tighten the former.

His family was middle-class, cultivated, Anglican. The

1

father was an amateur poet as well as the author of *A Manual of Marine Insurance* and *The Cardinal Numbers*. The mother read German philosophy. Aunt Hopkins taught him folk songs and Elizabethan airs. Of his three sisters,—one sketched well, another played the piano; the eldest became an Anglican nun. Three of his four brothers drew, two of them professionally, for *Punch*.

Both aesthete and ascetic appeared early. As a child, Gerard sobbed at the ugliness of his younger brother, disfigured by mumps or measles; lay abed one night horribly fascinated by "Hopkins": he later comforted himself by reflecting that he might have been born "Gerard Manley Tuncks." But the rigorist, meanwhile, practised tests of the will, chastisements of the soft, self-indulgent body. At boarding school, he denied himself salt for a week; another time he went for a week without drinking water or any other liquid, carrying out the bet he had made, though collapsing at the end of it. This test had been incited by schoolboy talk about the hardships and the endurance of sailors. Hopkins had all his days not only the cerebral man's admiration for sailors and soldiers and miners, but the need to show he could, in his own world and way, live as hard and dangerously.

In 1863, Hopkins, then nineteen, became an Oxford undergraduate. The "influences" upon him were various, rich: Jowett of Balliol, Hopkins' own college; Walter Pater, who was one of his tutors and had a special liking for him; Ruskin and William Morris (*daemones loci*); Pusey and H. P. Liddon, leaders in the Anglo-Catholic movement and the leading figures in Oxford Anglo-Catholicism. After a year of exploration, Hopkins found

2

his way into the group of Anglo-Catholic intellectuals, his special close circle of friends. He chose Liddon, an able theologian attractive to the young, as his confessor. He set himself specific ecclesiastical disciplines: "For Lent. No puddings on Sundays. No tea except if to keep me awake and then without sugar. No verses [presumably no composing of verses] in Passion week or on Fridays. Not to sit in armchair except can work no other way. Ash Wednesday and Good Friday bread and water." While still among the Anglicans, he wrote the first draught of "The Habit of Perfection," exquisite invocation and evocation of the ascetic life.

His Oxford friends were youths centrally concerned with religion. Their subsequent ecclesiastical careers have some typicality. Geldart, an Evangelical Anglican, became a Unitarian clergyman. Robert Bridges, later poet-laureate of England and Hopkins' posthumous editor, lost his religion. Vincent Coles remained an Anglo-Catholic, became Warden of Oxford's Pusey House. William Addis became a Roman Catholic in 1866 and a priest in 1872; returned to the English Church in 1901. The most "picturesque" of Hopkins' friends was a young Etonian, Digby Dolben, whose pattern has its similarities to those of Newman's Hurrell Froude and Emerson's Charles Newcomb. Before passing his examinations for Oxford or making his indicated submission to Rome, he died, at eighteen; but he had already written memorable poetry and become a tertiary of the Anglican Order of St. Benedict and walked, monastically robed and discalced, through the streets of Birmingham.

There survive Hopkins' Oxford diaries (or note-books,

3

—or *journals,* as Emerson would have called them), conceived as a double record,—secular (academic, aesthetic) and spiritual. The secular notes, from which a selection has been published by Mr. House, show Hopkins' eager perception of images and words, his appetite for detail, in nature and in architecture, his joy in the unique configuration of the sensuously transient which he called "inscape." There are delicate pen and ink sketches of trees, flowers, buildings, and architectural detail done in the manner of Ruskin. There are draughts of poems and lists of books to be read,—now, as for life, novels as well as poetry and theology: "The abundance of genius in English romance in his age appears to me comparable with its abundance in drama in the Elizabethan. . . ."

In October, 1866, Hopkins, still an undergraduate, was received into the Roman Catholic Church. The great Newman, whose *Apologia* had appeared in 1864 and whose *Difficulties of Anglicans* he had read, was the sign if not the means of his conversion. Before his reception, Hopkins wrote Newman and went to Birmingham for an interview; and thereafter, he felt a filial gratitude to his adviser, wrote him an annual birthday letter, wanted to edit his *Grammar of Assent.* Now Newman had sound advice as well as sympathy. "Your first duty is to make a good class [in the Oxford examinations]. Show your friends at home that your becoming a Catholic has not unsettled you in the plain duty that lies before you." Thus exhorted, Hopkins left Oxford, in June 1867, with a Double First in Greats [1] and Jowett's judgment that he was the star of Balliol, one of the finest of its Greek scholars.

[1] Of "Greats," or *Literae Humaniores,* at Oxford there is an excellent account in Sir R. W. Livingstone's "The Position and Func-

4

A BIOGRAPHICAL NOTE

The priesthood and indeed entry into some religious order seemed clear calls. Over which order he hesitated, but not for long. He rejected the gentlemanly and humanist Benedictines and Oratorians (the latter of Newman's foundation) for the military Jesuits; and he was reassured by Newman that he had made the right choice. "Don't call the Jesuit discipline 'hard'; it will bring you to heaven."

In September, 1868, he entered the Jesuit Novitiate, at Manresa House, Roehampton, just outside of London, to begin his nine years of training. He was a novice from 1868 to 1870, when he took his first vows and started three years of philosophical studies at Stonyhurst (1870–73). For a year he returned to Manresa House to teach classics. There followed three years of theological studies at St. Beuno's College in North Wales. In 1877 he was ordained. Then for four years he served as parish priest and preacher at Chesterfield, at the Farm St. Church in London, at Oxford, at Bedford Leigh, a gloomy mill and coal-mining town near Manchester, at Liverpool, at Glasgow. In 1881, he re-entered Manresa House, to pursue his ninth year of training, his "tertianship" or "Second Novitiate," during which he, like all Jesuits about to take their final vow, made a ten months' retirement from the education of the intellect and from active work in the world in order to re-examine motivations and to school the affections.

His superiors evidently decided that his future usefulness to the Order lay rather in teaching than in the cure of souls or parish administration. After two years as instructor in Latin and Greek at Stonyhurst, he was (in 1884)

tion of Classical Studies in Modern English Education," in the 1930–1 *Vorträge der Bibliothek Warburg* (ed. Saxe, Leipzig, 1932), 251 ff.

appointed to the chair of classics at University College, Dublin, the residue of Newman's efforts in behalf of a Catholic university. The "chair" was accompanied by a fellowship at the degree-granting Royal University, which required Hopkins to make out, correct, and grade semi-annual examinations in Greek.

Neither as parish priest nor as teacher was he successful by ordinary professional standards.

As priest, he was tried in well assorted parishes—fashionable Farm St., intellectual Oxford, working-class Liverpool and Glasgow. Preaching at Farm St., he amazed and amused the audience by comparing the sacramental Church to a cow with full udders inviting the needy stranger to milk it. At Liverpool, one July night he preached, seemingly with affective power; but he misinterpreted what he saw. In a sentence sounding like an ambiguity of Kafka, he wrote: "I thought people must be quite touched by this consideration and that I even saw some wiping their tears, but when the same thing happened next week I perceived that it was hot and that it was sweat they were wiping away." He tried preaching with and without manuscript. He grew nervous and confused in the pulpit.

Six of his sermons have been published (in *Note-books and Papers*). They are brilliant, eloquent, baroque discourses worthy of the poet who wrote them,—sermons to go with those of Andrewes, Donne, Taylor. They would have been better understood by a Jacobean congregation than by a Victorian. Yet they are not, like those of the Jacobean divines, aimed at educated gentlemen. They are not "university sermons," like Platonist John Smith's and

6

Newman's, addressing professed intellectuals and offering them a philosophy of religion. They postulate a probably non-existent congregation of unschooled but imaginative workingmen,—Felix Randall and Harry Ploughman.

Hopkins liked best his proletarian parishioners. While he was still studying at Stonyhurst, he wrote of himself to his friend Bridges, as "in a manner . . . a Communist. Their ideal, bating some things, is nobler than that professed by any secular statesman I know of. . . . Besides it is just.—I do not mean the means of getting to it are. But it is a dreadful thing for the greatest and most necessary part of a very rich nation to live a hard life without dignity, knowledge, comforts, delight, or hopes in the midst of plenty—which plenty they make." Much later, he wrote his friend Dixon: "My Liverpool and Glasgow experience laid upon my mind a conviction, a truly crushing conviction, of the misery of the town life to the poor and more than to the poor, of the misery of the poor in general, of the degradation of our race, of the hollowness of this century's civilization."

As a classical lecturer, he was unsuccessful in drawing or holding audiences,—in spite of an occasional divertissement like his dragging a student around the room to illustrate Patroclus' treatment of the dead Hector. Delicate and unworldly was his aversion to a required audience. He let it be known that he would not include in the examinations any topics discussed in his lectures: so the class, bent on passing the examination, not on mental culture, dwindled away.

The chief anxiety attended, and indeed anticipated, the

semi-annual reading of examinations,—hundreds of them. His "scrupulosity," his perfectionist desire to make no mistakes and to do injustice to no one, turned the final reckoning of these papers into a torture. To weigh his justice more precisely, he devised a grading in which each number was divided into halves and quarters; and at this weighing and balancing he toiled away till his eyes popped out of his head and his diarrhoea and vomiting brought a stop.

The whole vocation of professor he took with the same rigor. Though he was a poet, he judged that he must, as incumbent of a chair in Greek, be a publishing scholar or else betray the expectations and standards of a true University. In the Dublin years, accordingly, he conceived and wrote, or began to write, articles and books,—a "quasi-philosophical paper on the Greek Negatives," a book on the Dorian Measure in Greek lyric poetry, a paper on the lyrics of Aeschylus, an essay, "Readings and Renderings of Sophocles," an article on statistics and free will, an edition of St. Patrick's Confessions.

"Parish priest" and "teacher" were two of Hopkins' lives. He was also a scholar, a student of music, and a poet: it would require a catalogue to name all of his incipient selves. Over and beyond his professional activities and his poetic function, he had a lifelong, eager, restless curiosity to learn and do. While he was a student at St. Beuno's, he wanted to learn Welsh; then, upon self-examination, he decided that his central motive was not a passion to convert the Welsh from Methodism but philological pleasure; eventually, after adjustments, he received instruction in Welsh. Etymological speculations never ceased to inter-

8

est him,—the more if they concerned languages of which his knowledge was scant.

His concern with music was curious and characteristic. Shortly after leaving Oxford, he took up the violin briefly; he never learned the piano properly; yet in his Dublin years (while pressures increased) he began to teach himself harmony and counterpoint and to compose, sending his work to musicologists for correction but generally disputing their corrections. Hopkins' taste in music was, first of all for the pre-romantic English,—for Purcell, Blow, Storace, Linley, the 1764 ballad-opera *Midas;* but at the end he was moving towards the pre-classical and post-romantic. "Your music," a pianist said to his satisfaction, "comes from a time before the piano was." In 1885, he composed a modal setting for Collins' "Ode to Evening," about which he wrote to the musically minded Bridges, "It seems to me like a new art, the effect is so unlike anything I ever heard. The air is plainchant where plainchant [the liturgical music of the Church] most departs from modern music; on the other hand the harmonies are a kind of advance on advanced modern music. The combination of the two things is most singular, but it is also most solemn. . . ."

While still a schoolboy at Highgate, Hopkins wrote some obviously talented poems,—notably "A Vision of the Mermaids," after the manner of Keats. At Oxford, he felt the influence of Christina Rossetti and the male Pre-Raphaelites, whom he saw as the English representatives of new-mediaevalism. When he entered the Jesuit Order, he burned his old poems (as so many bridges back to the past) and resolved to write no more till he should, by

9

ecclesiastical authority, be enjoined to do so. After seven years (a round, symbolic number), the silence was lifted by a superior's suggestion that some member of the community should elegize the five Franciscan nuns who perished in the wreck of the "Deutschland."

When he began to write again, he wrote in a new way, putting on to paper a new rhythm which had long been haunting his ear. This was in 1875. Two years later, he sent it to Robert Bridges, his old Oxford friend, now an actively publishing poet. The next year, he began to correspond with a former master of his at school, an Anglican priest, church historian and poet, R. W. Dixon. For the rest of his life, Hopkins maintained close friendships with these two fellow-poets. The three exchanged poems and rigorous criticisms of poems as well as general literary intelligence. Bridges and Dixon could print their work but had small or non-existent audiences; Hopkins, partly because of his "advanced" style, partly because of his own scruples, could not be printed: Bridges and Canon Dixon, with occasional additions like the Catholic poet Patmore, were Hopkins' sole readers, readers of "imperfect sympathies."

The business of fame, that "last infirmity of noble minds," was a persistent disturbance which Hopkins could not settle. A Jesuit should not covet personal glory; careers he should have put behind him. Yet how can an artist keep on working without the hope of society's response? Indeed, does his art not otherwise become a kind of private indulgence? Hopkins urged his friends to write for their fame and England's glory while he found it his own duty to renounce such expectations.

A BIOGRAPHICAL NOTE

Hopkins' sad case has turned into something like a *cause célèbre,* in which Christianity, the Catholic Church and the Jesuits figure as damagers of his life and diminishers if not destroyers of his poetry. One view has it that Hopkins was some kind of Catholic Modernist (like Tyrrell), who never really accepted Catholic dogma. Another view is that the "terrible sonnets," written in the Dublin desolation, express the torment of a man who is losing faith in religion, tormentedly doubtful of the existence of God.

Both of these views are a priori constructions for which there is no producible evidence from Hopkins' letters and poems. The allegation of Modernism may partly have been occasioned by his devotion to Duns Scotus (about which, whether eccentric or not, there was nothing heretical). Chiefly, however, it must be due to Hopkins' very personal and unprofessional way of preaching and writing (the wonderful "Comments on the Spiritual Exercises," for example). But all the best Catholic writing has this freshness of idiom:—Pascal, Newman, Chesterton, Péguy. Yet the very freshness and independence, in turn, call up the rejoinder of the naturalist: "Minds of such originality can't be imagined really to believe in the incredible, banal old doctrines." All "thinking people" believe that all other thinkers believe as they: apparent exceptions are either insane or hypocrites. A "Puseyite" in his youth, later emancipated from dogmatic religion, Bridges apparently had to suppose Hopkins had just not acknowledged a like change in himself. Writing his old friend in 1882, of Latin hymns and ecclesiastical processions, Hopkins says: "It is long since such things had any significance for you. But what is strange and unpleasant

11

is that you sometimes speak as if they had in reality none for me and you were only waiting with a certain disgust till I too should be disgusted with myself enough to throw off the mask."

The "terrible sonnets" are not revelations of atheist face beneath Catholic mask. They are the cries of a pious soul undergoing *vastation, spiritual dryness,* feeling abandoned by God and unprofitable to self or Him. The images evoked are those of Jacob wrestling with the angel, the veiled God; of Job, believing in God but puzzled by the gap between piety and prosperity; of the prophet Jeremiah, from whom Hopkins quotes the epigraph over No. 50: "Righteous art thou, O Lord, when I plead with thee: Yet let me talk with thee of thy judgments: Wherefore doth the way of the wicked prosper?"

"Nervous prostration" was a medical phrase which named the outermost matter of these sonnets. To be unable to create, except rarely and sparsely, to be "time's eunuch," an unprofitable servant was one torment; the inability to finish projects, of which so many appear in the letters, another; there were the constant fatigue, the weakness, the sense of premature age, the melancholy, which he had (in the words of his late letter to Baillie) all his life been subject to but which had become "rather more distributed, constant, and crippling," its lightest form a "daily anxiety about work to be done. . . ."

The "spiritual sense" of these sonnets is the attempt to offer this psychic breakdown, this failure of the self's hopes and ambitions, including its ambitions to do good, on the altar of the Hidden God. The sonnet numbered 40 offers the dramatic monologue of the soul's wrestling with the God who permits this torture. The "anatomy" of the opening lines rejects the nauseously fascinating pleasure of giving in to Despair, the vice contrary to the "theological virtue" of Hope, the vice which, as *acedia,* is the spiritual form of the Deadly Sin of sloth, the vice which, in the judgment of some Fathers, is the "sin against the Holy Ghost." Despair says, "I can't"; suggests suicide as ease from the pain of inability. In the extreme desolation of "breakdown," it is the minimal necessary virtue to resist the voices of despair. . . .

> Not, I'll not, carrion comfort, Despair; not feast on thee;
> Not untwist—slack they may be—these last strands of man
> In me, or, most weary, cry *I can no more.* I can;
> Can something, hope, wish day come, not choose not to be.

Fr. D'Arcy doubts that Hopkins would have recovered from his breakdown had he lived, seems to make no connection between Hopkins' "scrupulosity" and his breakdown (which is viewed as purely constitutional, physical). Precarious as it is to make the proper linkages and translations between the somatic, the psychic and the spiritual, I should suppose all breakdowns in maturity to be ultimately spiritual, testifying to the finite self's unwillingness to acknowledge its creatureness, its clinging to known securities instead of plunging itself gladly into the abyss of God. Accordingly I should be unable to reconcile irrecoverable breakdown with saintliness.[2]

Neither Catholicism nor his order crippled Hopkins. The Jesuits did not ask him to burn his pre-Jesuit poems or

[2] "Neurosis and true saintliness are incompatible." "Beyond the neurotic there stands only the saint." R. Allers, *Psychology of Character* (1939), 298, 326.

13

to write no poetry till bidden by authority or to refuse publication or to eschew poetry in favor of classical philology: those were Hopkins' own interpretations of his duty as priest and Jesuit. If he never, as it would seem, found a spiritual director who centrally understood his nature and its problems, he was, it is clear, treated with ordinary good sense. His superiors handled him indulgently,—tried to find suitable scope for his talents, gave him frequent vacations, respected his fine integrity.

My own conclusion is that Hopkins' constant tension, the desire to be an artist and the desire to be a saint, was necessary to his achievement as a poet. Had he written with the facility and fecundity of most Victorians (his friends included) he might have been as undistinguished. He had early ease; he needed to learn to write under difficulty,—to theorize, ponder, wait more often than compose. The inhibitions came; and consequently the small body of Hopkins' work, like that of Eliot, offers a series of poetic stances, every important poem constituting a new mode.

There are two polar types of poet,—the "maker," or craftsman, and the self-explorer who renovates the art through work on himself and the language,—from the Romantic movement, the type of our best poets. Hopkins is a curious case of "maker" moving, by force of his tension, into self-explorer.

This poetically fruitful tension was doubtless one of the causes of Hopkins' breakdown. The best poetry is costly. Had he recovered from his breakdown, it might have been by ceasing to write, passing again into silence. Even a literary man can imagine a sanctity oblivious of art.

14

2. THE ANALOGICAL MIRRORS

By Herbert Marshall McLuhan

HOPKINS IS FULL OF PITFALLS FOR THE UNWARY. THERE IS A double difficulty: his Catholic beliefs and experience on one hand; his individual use of the resources of English on the other, to say nothing of his irrelevant theory of prosody. The non-Catholic reader—especially the non-Christian reader—is timid or hostile in the presence of Hopkins' faith and doctrine. He is beset with "mnemonic irrelevance" and stirred to a thousand acts of undemanded vigilance and depreciation which inevitably distort the pattern and texture of the poems.

For the Catholic reader Hopkins has, understandably, a great deal of prestige value. Long accustomed to a defensive position behind a minority culture, English and American Catholics have developed multiple mental squints. Involuntarily their sensibilities have been nourished and ordered by a century or more of an alien literary

15

and artistic activity which, *faute de mieux,* they still approach askance. However, their intellectual distrust in the presence of, say, the emotional chaos of Shelley or Browning has not in the least prevented the assimilation of the vision of those poets. (One might add that it has not in the least prevented them from hailing as "Catholic poetry" the febrile immaturities of Francis Thompson and Joyce Kilmer.)

Thus there was no Catholic magazine which would accept any poem of Hopkins in his lifetime. With Bloomsbury's sudden acclaim of Hopkins as a major poet, however, Catholics were caught off-guard. They hastened to enshrine but not to understand him. Somewhat inconsequentially they have begun to feel at home in the present world of art because "their" poet is a big gun on the literary front. That is the catch. The Catholic reader comes to Hopkins with a mechanism of sensibility which came off the line in 1850. His sensibility has been unmodified by the impact of Baudelaire, Laforgue, Pound or Eliot. Bloomsbury was at least readied for Hopkins by these and *The Seafarer.* But the Catholic assumes his proprietary manner on the strength of doctrinal affinity alone. With equal justification the professors of Anglo-Saxon might have staked out an exclusive claim in Hopkins. Insentience or modesty has prevented them so far; or is it simply that they are incapable of seeing that the work of Hopkins is almost the sole civilized fruit of their brain-starved plodding?

Before there can be any basis for Catholic complacency in the presence of Hopkins we must explain our tardy recognition of him. Again, if Catholic doctrine made Hopkins a major poet, why aren't there more like him? All, I think, that need be said of this peculiarly Catholic pitfall is that some knowledge (the more the better) of Catholic doctrines and Scotist philosophy is needed for the full elucidation, though not for the immediate enjoyment, of Hopkins. Such knowledge, however, will never reveal his poetic excellence. The Catholic reader has the advantage only in that he is disposed to give Hopkins a chance. And, of course, he is not inclined to urp, with Bridges, when Hopkins speaks of the Virgin or the Trinity. The problem, in short, is much the same as that of reading, say, Dante or John Donne. The ancillary scholarly effort should, but seldom does, keep ever sharply focussed the stereoscopic gaze at the work itself.

Before looking at "The Windhover," as our chosen text, let us consider the crux of Hopkins' sensibility—"inscape." It is the "fineness, proportion of feature" mastering the recalcitrance of matter which he saw everywhere in the world. It is the ontological secret:

> It is the forgèd feature finds me; it is the rehearsal
> Of own, of abrupt self there so thrusts on, so throngs the ear.

Hopkins finds this Euclid peeping from the chaos of matter alike in the veins of a violet, the "roped" sides of a mountain, or the bright shoe on the anvil. (Note the precise yet witty implications of "forged feature" in this connection.) That Hopkins should take the further step of greeting Christ at such moments of natural perception should cause even the non-Catholic reader very little inconvenience, for the poet is making no pantheistic claims whatever:

17

Since, tho' he is under the world's splendour and wonder,
His mystery must be instressed, stressed.

Hopkins is not a nature mystic at all, nor a religious mystic, either, but an analogist. By stress and instress, by intensity and precision of perception, by analogical analysis and meditation he achieves all his effects. His is literally a sacramental view of the world since what of God is there he does not perceive nor experience but takes on faith. It may sound at first strange to hear that Hopkins is not a mystic but an analogist. That he does not lay claim to a perception of natural facts hidden from ordinary men is evident in every line of description he ever wrote. As for religious experience, it is the same. Nowhere in his work does he draw on an experience which is beyond the range of any thoughtful and sensitive Catholic who meditates on his Faith. Let the authoritative statement of Jacques Maritain clarify this matter at once. He begins a chapter on "Expérience Mystique et Philosophie" this way:

Nous entendrons ici le mot "expérience mystique," que cela soit convenu une fois pour toutes, non pas en un sens plus ou moins vague (extensible à toutes sortes de faits plus ou moins mystérieux ou préternaturels, ou même à la simple religiosité), mais au sens de *connaissance expérimentale* des profondeurs de Dieu, ou de *passion des choses divines,* menant l'âme, par une suite d'états et de transformations, jusqu'à éprouver au fond d'elle-même le toucher de la déité, et à "sentir la vie de Dieu." *Les Degrés Du Savoir* (Paris, 1935), pp. 489–490.

But there is nothing of this in Hopkins. He deals sensitively with the commonplaces of Catholic dogma in the order of Faith, and he records a vigorous sensuous life

18

in the order of nature. Since for the agnostic no precision is possible in these matters, and all distinctions are nugatory, he will continue to call both Blake and Hopkins "mystical."

Hopkins looks at external nature as a Scripture exactly as Philo Judaeus, St. Paul and the Church Fathers had done. Their views, which have never ceased to be current, though their prevalence has fluctuated, are summarily expressed by the conventional patristic divine, Jeremy Taylor:

Thus when (God) made the beauteous frame of heaven and earth, he rejoyced in it, and glorified himself, because it was the glasse in which he beheld his wisdom, and Almighty power: . . . For if God is glorified in the Sunne and Moon, in the rare fabric of the honeycombs, in the discipline of Bees, in the œconomy of Pismires, in the little houses of birds, in the curiosity of an eye, God being pleased to delight in those little images and reflexes of himself from those pretty mirrours, which like a crevice in a wall thorow a narrow perspective transmit the species of a vast excellency: much rather shall God be pleased to behold himself in the glasses of our obedience. . . .

Hopkins habitually shifts his gaze from the order and perspectives of nature to the analogous but grander scenery of the moral and intellectual order. And he does this methodically:

> . . . O the mind, mind has mountains; cliffs of fall
> Frightful, sheer, no-man-fathomed.

Or the book of nature provides parallel passages with the supernatural revelations of Scripture:

> . . . For Christ plays in ten thousand places,
> Lovely in limbs and lovely in eyes not his
> To the Father through the features of men's faces.

As the microcosm of man is a nobler, a more perfect mirror of God's beauty and grandeur, so Christ, as Taylor goes on to say in the same place, "was the image of the Divinity . . . designed from eternal ages to represent as in a double mirrour, not onely the glories of God to himself, but also to all the world; and he glorified God by the instrument of obedience, in which God beheld his own dominion. . . ." Hopkins freely employs these three traditional mirrors (physical, moral, divine) of God's beauty and grandeur, using them sometimes simply ("Pied Beauty"), doubly ("The Caged Skylark"), or triply ("The Wreck of the Deutschland"). Naturally, these combinations admit of infinite variations since the particulars reflected in each "mirror" can be chosen from a great store.

"The Windhover" exploits all three mirrors of God's grandeur.

I caught this morning morning's minion, king-
  dom of daylight's dauphin, dapple-dawn-drawn Falcon, in his
  riding
 Of the rolling level underneath him steady air, and striding
High there, how he rung upon the rein of a wimpling wing
In his ecstasy! then off, off forth on swing,
  As a skate's heel sweeps smooth on a bow-bend: the hurl and
  gliding
 Rebuffed the big wind. My heart in hiding
Stirred for a bird,—the achieve of, the mastery of the thing!

Brute beauty and valour and act, oh, air, pride, plume, here
  Buckle! AND the fire that breaks from thee then, a billion
Times told lovelier, more dangerous, O my chevalier!

  No wonder of it: shéer plód makes plough down sillion
Shine, and blue-bleak embers, ah my dear,
  Fall, gall themselves, and gash gold-vermillion.

20

THE ANALOGICAL MIRRORS

The bird "literally" mirrors the physical order of sub-rational "valour and act." But, analogously, as "kingdom of daylight's dauphin," it mirrors Christ. As Hopkins transfers his gaze from the first mirror to the second, we see that his own heart is also a hidden mirror (moral obedience) which flashes to God the image not of "brute beauty and valour and act" but a "fire" which is "a billion times told lovelier"—the chevalier image of Christ. We can thus simply, and, I believe for the first time, fully explain the function of "here Buckle!" Rhetorically, fire bursts from Hopkins as he looks at the fiery falcon whose action mirrors the mastery of Christ over the world. Now, he says, let us take this mirror (St. Paul's "armour") and buckle it here in my hidden heart, raising the image of Christ in the bird to the image of Christ in the obedience and humility of the heart. Christ's fire will burst on and from the second mirror "a billion times told lovelier" than from the falcon. This is the basic structure of this image. The superstructure of its ambiguity will be shown later on. Hopkins would even seem to have this mirror mechanism in the forefront of his mind as he compares his obedient day-by-day plodding to the homely ploughshare whose polished surface is hidden in the earth ("my heart in hiding") but which imparts a sheen even to the mud and dirt which it turns up. (Compare with this "sheer plod" image "the jading and jar of the cart"—"Deutschland," stanza 27.)

To have seen the dialectic or mechanism of the poem is not, however, to have seen anything of what constitutes its dramatic action. In other words, we have yet to see that it is a poem at all. There is a logical movement which has been indicated. There is also dramatic surprise achieved by a striking peripeteia. This happens when the ecstatic hyperboles of the octet are yet rendered trite by the merely homely images of the sestet. Moreover, while the sestet is in a lower key, befitting the change to the theme of humble obedience, it is more intense, fuller of compressed implication. Hopkins has Spiritual humility act out its easy victory over "brute beauty and valour and act." Yet this victory is not won by crushing "brute beauty" but by catching it to the hidden heart which reflects it back to God.

The assonance and alliteration in the first three lines perform just the opposite of their usual functions in Hopkins' verse—the opposite of "gall" and "gash" in the last line, for example. Here, in conjunction with the even phrasing, they convey the delicate poise, the hovering emphasis of the falcon's movements. The falcon is seen as a chevalier, a horseman glorying in the great power under him and the quick response to the rein as he sweeps "forth on swing." (The skate on ice image shifts the point of view only to stress the precision and sharply etched movements of the bird. Compare: "It is the forgèd feature finds me" in "Henry Purcell." "Dapple-dawn-drawn Falcon" also insists upon the etched quality of the scene. The bird is drawn to the light but it is also drawn, etched, against the dawn.)

To a member of a militant order whose founder was a Spanish soldier or chevalier, the feudal character of the opening imagery is quite natural. "Minion," "dauphin," "valour," "plume" and "buckle" alike evoke the world of dedicated knighthood and shining panoply of armor. Thus

22

the mounted chevalier flashing off exploit as he "rung upon the rein" enables Hopkins later to reverse the situation with great dramatic effect in "sheer plod makes plow down sillion Shine." The paradox consists in the fact that Hopkins as lowly plowman following a horse flashes off infinitely more exploit than Hopkins the imagined chevalier.

More central still to the dramatic movement of the poem is the way in which the cavalier images of the octet are concentrated in "here Buckle!" Buckling is the traditional gesture of the knight preparing his armor for action. A buckler is the bright shield of defense bearing insignia, flashing defiance. (The relevance of the sense of "buckle" as "collapse" or "crumple" has often been debated in this context. It has been suggested that Hopkins, in shifting his point of view, here means that the sensuous beauty of the world is a feeble prop, that he is making a conventional renunciation of "mortal beauty" as dangerous to the spiritual life. But this is to ignore the dramatic development, to blur it with cliché. It ignores the excited emphasis of "here" at the end of the line and "Buckle!" at the beginning of the next. It is, of course, almost impossible not to accept these suggestions so long as the basic mirror images of his analogist vision are not grasped.) Whichever way one looks at this image the implication of shining brilliance, of enthusiastic gesture, is present. I have already said that "here" means "in the obedient and humble heart," and that "Buckle" means that the "brute beauty" of the bird as mirror of God's grandeur is to be transferred or flashed to the "heart in hiding," just as the burnished surface of the plow in action is hidden in the earth. The high-

23

spirited but obedient heart of a man is a "billion Times" better a mirror of Christ the chevalier than is the mirror of the external world. "AND the fire that breaks from thee then" (note how the eager stress on "AND" serves to flash attention intensely on what follows as being an inevitable result) is ambivalent in suggesting both the fire and ecstasy which the poet has felt as he watched the bird as well as the much greater fire which Christ will flash on him and from him, and which will flame out at the world. The mirror of man's moral life can "give beauty back to God," the beauty of God's world, and in so doing it becomes the mirror in which (by the imitation of Christ) God can flash out more brilliantly. ("Give beauty back," as in a mirror, is also the theme of "The Leaden Echo and the Golden Echo," as the title suggests.)

Once it is seen that the shining armor of the falcon's imitation of Christ's mastery is to be buckled in the hidden heart of the poet it is easy to find other passages in Hopkins which show that this image obsessed him. In the sonnet to St. Alphonsus Rodriguez there is the same running image of military brilliance and valor:

> But be the war within, the brand we wield
> Unseen, the heroic breast not outward-steeled,
> Earth hears no hurtle then from fiercest fray.

The whole sonnet is helpful to an understanding of "Windhover." But there is especial relevance in the second line:

> And those strokes that once gashed flesh or galled shield.

There is here a direct clue to the last lines of our poem.

24

> No wonder of it: shéer plód makes plough down sillion
> Shine, and blue-bleak embers, ah my dear,
> Fall, gall themselves, and gash gold-vermillion.

"Gall" and "gash" are in both places associated with shield and mirror and flesh—mortified or obedient flesh, of course. The underlying image in these last three lines is that of mortal *clay* transformed. It is made to shine and to fructify by the humble service of the plough (the obedient will). The "blue-bleak" earth provides the transition to the embers covered with clay-like ash. Just as "the fire that breaks from thee then" (after the mirror of mortal beauty has been buckled to the hidden heart) is not a fire produced by any direct action or valor, so the fire that breaks from the "blue-bleak embers" is not the effect of *ethos* but *pathos*, not of action but of suffering or patience. The true "achieve of, the mastery of the thing" from which flashes the most dangerous and daring exploit

> dates from day
> Of his going in Galilee
> Warm-laid grave of a womb-life grey;

Here again is the image of the fire in the hidden heart which evokes the "blue-bleak embers," and, which, as some have suggested, leads on to the image of the vermillion side of Christ on the Cross.

One might even suggest that as the ash-covered coals gash gold-vermillion when touched by the poker (spear), so when Hopkins "kissed the rod, Hand rather" ("Carrion Comfort"), he becomes a mirror of Christ, flashing gold-vermillion:

I kissed the rod,
Hand rather, my heart lo! lapped strength,
Stole joy, would laugh, chéer.
Cheer whom though? the hero whose heaven-handling
flung me, fóot tród
Me? or me that fought him?

The *crucial* ambivalence which Hopkins stresses is owing to the double mirror image which he keeps always in mind. As a mirror of Christ he must imitate both the valor and also the obscure sufferings of Christ. He must overcome and be overcome at the same instant—at every instant. But this complexity does not exist in the mirror of mortal beauty, the "brute beauty and valour and act" which is a simple reflection of Christ's mastery but not of His suffering and love.

Familiarity with Hopkins soon reveals that each of his poems includes all the rest, such is the close-knit character of his sensibility. A relatively small number of themes and images—such is the intensity of his perception—permits him an infinitely varied orchestration. Thus it is really impossible to feel the full impact of "The Windhover" without awareness of the tentacles which its images stretch out into the other poems. To take once more the analogy of "sheer plod makes plough down sillion Shine," its paradox is brightly illuminated in the poem "That Nature is a Heraclitean Fire." Contemplating his "joyless days, dejection," "flesh fade, and mortal trash," he reflects that:

This Jack, joke, poor potsherd, patch, matchwood, immortal diamond,
Is immortal diamond.

This "Jack, joke" plodding behind the plough makes the

trash and mud of earth shine like diamond, "wafting him out of it." And diamond flashing from the silicates of the soil is also, once again, the mirror of Christ in the hidden and humble heart of mortal clay.

Another aspect of this analogy of the plough grinding through the gritty soil is seen in the last line of "Spelt from Sybil's Leaves":

Where, selfwrung, selfstrung, sheathe- and shelterless, thóughts agáinst thoughts in groans grínd.

This aspect of the plough and the soil is the more obviously dramatic one—immortal beauty won from the harshest dullest toil, suffering and discipline.

An inevitable dispersal of attention has accompanied the above elucidation of this poem. But then only an oral reading with all the freedom and flexibility of spoken discussion can really point to the delicate interaction, at each moment of the poem, of all its cumulative vitality of logic, fancy, musical gesture.

"The Windhover" could never have become the richly complex poem it is if Hopkins had not tested and explored all its themes beforehand, in other poems. There is no other poem of comparable length in English, or perhaps in any language, which surpasses its richness and intensity or realized artistic organization. There are two or three sonnets of Shakespeare (for example, "They that have power to hurt" and "The expense of spirit") which might be put with Donne's "At the round earth's" for comparison and contrast with this sonnet. But they are not comparable with the range of the experience and multiplicity of integrated perception which is found in "The Windhover."

3. SPRUNG RHYTHM

By Harold Whitehall

A POET'S THEORIES ARE NOT ALWAYS THE BEST GUIDE TO HIS poetry. Wordsworth should not be judged solely from the "Preface" to the *Lyrical Ballads,* nor Sidney Lanier from his *Science of English Verse.* Many an admirer of Mr. Eliot, the poet, has been more discouraged than aided by the revelations of Mr. Eliot, the critic. Not so with Gerard Manley Hopkins. His is the almost unique case of a poet who preached what he practised and practised what he preached. As the voluminous comments in his *Letters* show, his verse conforms to a thesis—a metrical thesis. Understand the thesis, and you grasp his poetic purpose; grasp his purpose, and you have the key to his poems.

This metrical thesis is no simple question of stressed and unstressed syllables. Far more than modern criticism recognizes, it is a cortical strand in the personal tragedy of Hopkins, the man. At the heart of that tragedy, as his letters show, lies artistic loneliness—loneliness no measure of good will could ever dissipate, loneliness made intolerable by the sympathetic but unintuitive good will of Dixon, Bridges and his other friends. His genius for friendship merely intensified his isolation; he needed not friendship, but a friendly insight capable of penetrating the quickset of obscurities and contradictions which invested his poetic theories. In the beginning, he was sure that the insight was there. Then, completely disillusioned, he pursued a belligerent defensive—immersed himself in prosodic and linguistic studies to justify his metrical innovations to his friends. Towards the end, he was obliged in part to renounce his innovations, his theories, his defense, and even the very practice of poetry itself.

This is not to deny other influences on his poetic life. I should not wish to underestimate his increasing preoccupation with musical composition nor to minimize his religious vocation and its effects on the spirit and substance of his poetry. But his ultimate tragedy—a very real and moving tragedy—seems to spring from his deep sense of poetic failure. There is more than passing significance in a remark to Bridges (*Letters* I. cxxxvi):

What are works of art for? to educate, to be standards. To produce is of little use unless what we produce is known, is widely known, the wider known the better, for it is by being known that it works, it influences, it does its duty, it does good. We must try, then, to be known, aim at it, take means to it. And this without puffing in the process or pride in the success. . . . Besides, we are Englishmen. A great work by an Englishman is like a great battle won for England.

These are brave words. As written by a poet unknown in his own day, destined to gain a severely limited audience

ten years after posthumous publication, to influence an
alien generation of cerebral poets, and to serve as a poetic
yardstick for the analytical subtlety of certain modern in-
tellectuals, they rank among the major ironies of English
literature.

Every poet bears partial responsibility for his own fail-
ures. Hopkins may be blamed for his own insufficient un-
derstanding of the nature of "sprung rhythm" and for the
defensive vacillations which produced theoretical confu-
sion (Cp. *Letters* II. v, xii, xxi; I. xxxvii, xxxxix, lxix, lxxi,
and the "Preface" to his *Poems*). He cannot be blamed for
the key difficulty—that few of his friends had ever heard
him read poems aloud. For them, for him, and for his mod-
ern admirers, however, the trouble goes deeper than that
—goes deep as the very roots of English versification. Be-
hind his own confusion and the honest bewilderment of
Bridges, Dixon and Patmore looms the whole trend of
English verse from *circa* 1300 to the present: its increasing
emphasis of the sense pattern rather than the sound pat-
tern; its gradual assimilation to conditions of the printed,
rather than the spoken or chanted, word; its exodus from
the crowded hall to the quiet library, from public per-
formance to private perusal. If this can excuse the critical
shortcomings of Hopkins' Victorian contemporaries, fam-
iliar as they were with the romantic medievalism of the
Pre-Raphaelite era, how much more will it excuse those
modern poet-critics who, in Mr. Read's phrase, ascend
Parnassus by the dry gullies of intellect.

Not that one can quarrel with the progress of English
verse. Granted the molding force of the printed word,
poetry must inevitably slough off its musical integument

and attain a form for which mute-lipped reading is the ultimate artistic realization. Experimentalist modern verse—a verse which substitutes ideational for stress-durational rhythms and connotational for aural overtones—is merely the latest phase in a development several centuries old. When a poet like Hopkins, coming towards the end of this development, echoes the poetic procedures of its earliest stages, he is bound to be judged by canons of taste not strictly applicable to his work; inevitably, his sound-pattern poetry is appraised as though it were sense-pattern poetry. Critics of our own time and his are necessarily accustomed to a type of verse which, whatever its intellectual or emotional subtleties, is at least rhythmically straightforward. What critical standards can their contemporary experience suggest for verse written by a metrical virtuoso for virtuosic performance *aloud?* It is useless to insist, as Hopkins insisted, on the poems being *heard*—to demand from the reader of poetry the same arduous preparation that Paderewski gave to a Liszt concerto or an Old English gleeman to *Beowulf*. Old habit dies hard. The generations of easy-to-read poets have taken their inevitable toll. The virtuosity that demands aural and oral bravura from both poet and performer is pre-judged, and often misjudged, by the criticism of the eye alone.

Hopkins' verse is not, and was never intended to be, closet verse. It reaches ultimate expression as poetry only when performed by a skilled reader before an audience capable of appreciating its phonal and rhythmical subtleties. On this point the poet himself is insistent. In *Letters* I. cxliii (referring to "Spelt from Sibyl's Leaves"), he says:

Of this long sonnet above all remember what applies to all my verse, that it is, as living art should be, made for performance and that its performance is not reading with the eye but loud, leisurely, poetical (not rhetorical) recitation, with long rests, long dwells on the rhyme and other marked syllables, and so on. This sonnet shd. be almost sung: it is most carefully timed in *tempo rubato*.

And again (I. lix):

Everybody cannot be expected to like my pieces. Moreover the oddness may make them repulsive at first sight. . . . Indeed, when, on somebody returning to me my *Eurydice*, I opened and read some lines, reading, as one commonly reads whether prose or verse, with the eyes, so to say, only, it struck me aghast with a kind of raw nakedness and unmitigated violence I was unprepared for; but take breath and read it with the ears, as I always wish to be read, and my verse becomes right.

No wonder that Hopkins' friends, and our contemporaries to whom performance poetry means "The Green Eye of the Yellow God" and "The Congo," have mistaken his poetic intention. The wonder is that he ever found any audience at all. Whatever its immediate sources, Hopkins' poetic aim is that of the Old and Middle English alliterative poets, of the authors of the Irish *droighneach* and Norse Skaldic verses, of Langland, Lagamon, the "Pearl Poet," and the anonymous master who wrote "The Wanderer." None of these would have encountered any considerable difficulty in Hopkins' external poetic forms. Our difficulty springs from our modernity, which, like all modernities, is both self-complacent and self-limited.

The complexities and obscurities in Hopkins' verse we try to elucidate from our experience with contemporary verse—a verse intellectually complex but symbolically simple; organically unified through single well-wrought analogies; incapable, for the most part, of the rush of diverse images found in earlier English poetry. Because contemporary verse supposedly thrusts aside traditional rhythmic and stanzaic forms for "freedom of expression," we regard Hopkins as an isolated pioneer breaking through the barriers of language to attain directness and precision of thought. Some of us have even murmured that he added decisive impetus to the revolutionary movement inaugurated by Wordsworth, furthered by the Victorian "common-speech" poets, and enormously developed by British and American experimentalists of the twenties and thirties. All this in spite of the plain evidence of Hopkins' *Letters* and *Notebooks*.

2

Hopkins' own explanations of his metrical theories can be assembled from several sources: from numerous letters to Patmore, Dixon, Bridges and Baillie (especially I. xxxv, xxxvii, xxxix; II. iii, v, xii and xxxiiic); from the "Essay on Rhythm and Other Structural Parts of Rhetoric" (*Notebooks*, pp. 241–248); and from the so-called "Author's Preface" written about 1883 for Bridges' MS.B. Of these sources, only the "Preface" contains the poet's most mature thought on his metrical problems. It postdates many significant references in the *Letters* and most of the important poems. In some particulars—notably in advocating scansion from the first stress of the line and the first stress of each foot—it contradicts all Hopkins' earlier statements. In spite of its omissions and its strange silences

33

on vital rhythmic matters, it contains the most illuminating exposition of Hopkins' theories.

He opens his remarks with the statement that his poems are written in *running rhythm* (elsewhere called *common rhythm*), in *sprung rhythm,* and, occasionally, in a combination of the two. Those in running rhythm may or may not be *counterpointed.* If running rhythm is scanned from the first stress of the line, it will be found to consist of accentual trochees and dactyls. When both occur together, the rhythm is *logaoedic,* or mixed. When two or more reversed feet occur consecutively within a line, the rhythm is counterpointed, *viz.,* the effect is produced of superimposing a new, or "mounted," rhythm upon the rhythm already established.

In Hopkins' view, the great master of English counterpointed rhythm is Milton, especially the Milton of the *Samson Agonistes* choruses; but since Milton often sets up the counterpoint before establishing his standard rhythm, many readers have mistaken his intention and found his verse irregular. Thus, what Milton actually writes absorbs all traces of the standard rhythm, ceases to be contrapuntal, and emerges as an entirely new type of rhythmic movement. This movement Hopkins calls "Sprung," i.e., abrupt. He then proceeds to summarize its characteristics in his own poems. Its external distinguishing feature is the free occurrence of juxtaposed stresses without intermediate unstressed syllables. It is measured in feet of one to four syllables, though for special effects the number of weak syllables may be unlimited. The stress falls on the only syllable of a monosyllabic foot and in other cases on the first syllable. The rhythm contains four types of feet:

34

"a monosyllable, and the so-called accentual Trochee, Dactyl, and the First Paeon." Normally, the lines are mixed, or logaoedic, and all types of feet are assumed to be of equal length, irrespective of the number of constituent syllables. Any seeming inequality is offset by pause and the strength of the stress. The scansion of sprung rhythm runs on without a break, from the beginning of the stanza to the end, the lines being *rove-over* (enjambed). Finally, the rhythm has two natural licenses: rests, as in music, and *hangers* or *outrides*, that is, "one, two, or three slack syllables added to a foot and not counted in the nominal scanning . . . so called because they seem to hang below the line or ride forward or backward from it in another dimension."

Obviously, Hopkins' descriptions of "running rhythm" contain nothing revolutionary. He expresses notions explicitly or implicitly recognized by all good English versifiers: that irregularity, as well as regularity, is a basic constituent of English rhythm; that rhythmic effectiveness depends upon the contrast between a well-established primary movement and a variation movement, both heard at the same time. This Hopkins calls *counterpoint*. He deserves credit for so clearly recognizing and describing its function; but the phenomenon is as old as the language, and it cannot be said of his ideas that they are either startlingly new or bewilderingly difficult.

If there are difficulties in his discussion of sprung rhythm, it is because his own analysis of its principles is incomplete. Thanks to an extremely sensitive ear, musical training, a close study of the rhythms of Milton and Campbell, and some acquaintance with Old English and Welsh,

35

Hopkins had stumbled upon a basic but hitherto unrecognized principle of rhythm—English or foreign, classical or modern. Consciously or subconsciously, he had come to realize that a metrical foot represents a unit in a series of even-time (isochronous) units and that, if these even-time units are in some manner marked off for the perception of the reader, their time-lapses may be occupied by anything from a single heavily-stressed syllable to four or five syllables. In short, granted a rhythmic regularity based upon even-time units, stress arrangements within the individual units can be varied almost at will.

Unfortunately, Hopkins slights the whole question of functional quality. His explanations are solely concerned with stress, with the variations of stress-pattern, and, particularly, with the occurrence of juxtaposed stresses; he ignores completely the principle of isochronous regularity which underlies the stress-variations. Although his manuscript contains whirls and loops, colons, accent marks, and brackets designed to show the minutiae of the stress system, he never mentions the far more effective marking of the time-units that his constant alliteration, assonance, internal rhyme, and word repetition provide. His sprung rhythm must be read as we read the words of a song when we happen to know the tune. If we do not know the tune—and Hopkins never furnishes it—the words may become, and in print frequently do become, a meaningless jumble of syllables.

Ironically enough, one at least of Hopkins' acquaintances had the metrical equipment to understand what he was about. Coventry Patmore's "Essay on English Metrical Law" shows a clear recognition of the system of isochronous time units. Its use of a musical scansion-notation between bar lines is precisely what Hopkins needed to convey his metrical intentions. Its central metrical thesis accords in theory with what Hopkins was attempting in practice. Patmore believes that the basic measure of English verse is a "dipody," that is to say, a measure, "double the measure of ordinary prose," containing the "space" bounded by alternate accents. He recognizes the time-marking function of secondary stress, realizes (like Poe) that the end measure of a line may be completed in the anacrusis of the next, and understands perfectly that the first stress of each dipody needs the extra emphasis given in older English poetry by alliteration.

Hopkins' sprung rhythm, and for that matter most of his running rhythm, follows Patmore's theories almost to the letter. Yet Patmore and Hopkins never saw how they complemented each other. Although Hopkins had undoubtedly read the Patmore essay by 1881 (*Letters* I. lxxi), he was too limited by conventional metrical theory and by concessions to stanzaic form to realize its bearing on the explanation of his own work. Patmore, for his part, had never heard Hopkins read his poems aloud, was puzzled by the appearance of the poems in Hopkins' manuscript (*Letters* I. cxiii), and was misled by the abrupt juxtaposition of stresses which is Hopkins' chief metrical innovation. If accidents of time and friendship had permitted an early meeting between the two men— the virtuosic dipodic practitioner and our first dipodic theorist—Hopkins' poems might have yielded their metrical secrets in his own lifetime. For all we know, such a

37

meeting might have led to immediate publication of Hopkins' verse, and to the infinite enriching of English lyric in even the Victorian period.

3

Hopkins provides a first clue to the real nature of sprung rhythm in one of his letters (I. xxxvii, February, 1878):

> Why do I employ sprung rhythm at all? Because it is nearest to the rhythm of prose, that is the native and natural rhythm of speech, the least forced, the most rhetorical and emphatic of all rhythms, combining it seems to me, opposite, and one wd. have thought, incompatible excellences, markedness of rhythm—that is rhythm's self—naturalness of expression. . . .

Now the "native and natural rhythm of speech" is by no means the rhythm suggested by conventional scansions of English verse. Conventional scansion abstracts from the speech flow only the factors of stress and lack of stress; it recognizes no quantitative factor whatsoever. Yet the instrumental phonetician can differentiate up to six degrees of stress and three degrees of syllabic juncture in English speech. Although instrumental and physical perception often differ sharply, the abstraction governing our metrics has obviously gone too far. Any dictionary gives three degrees of stress—strong, light, and zero. Any average perception has little difficulty in differentiating between the open and close juncture of contiguous syllables (e.g., *blackbird, washer*). Even on the perceptual level, therefore, the normal system of scansion ignores characteristics of the English language which are vital to the real understanding of English rhythm.

SPRUNG RHYTHM

These characteristics, of basic importance for Hopkins' metrics, can be best illustrated by examining English compounds and derivatives. *Honeysuckle,* for instance, contains four syllables with strong stress on the first, zero stress on the second and fourth, and light stress on the third: its stress pattern can be symbolized as SOLO; its syllabic junctures are all close. *Typewriter,* on the other hand, has strong stress on the first, light stress on the second, and zero stress on the third syllable: its stress pattern is SLO, with open juncture between the first and second syllables and close juncture between the second and third. *Blackbird* has the pattern SL, with open juncture; *polyphonic,* the pattern LOSO, with close juncture; *lilactime,* the pattern SOL, with close juncture. Combined, any four of these words will give lines of four well-defined sections or measures with a definite rhythmic movement:

```
Honeysuckle  lilactime  typewriter  blackbird
S  O  L  O / SOL / S L O /     S L
Honeysuckle  polyphonic  lilactime  blackbird
S  O  L  O / L O S O / S O L / S L
```

But stress-scansion alone ignores a basic constituent of the movement. The open junctures of *typewriter* and *blackbird* balance quantitatively the close-junctured *-ey, -le, -y, -ic,* and *-ac* of *honeysuckle, polyphonic,* and *lilactime.* When the quantitative value of the open juncture (p = pause) is put into the scansion, we can see at once that we have constructed dipodic lines of four even-time (isochronous) units:

```
S  O  L O / S O L p / S p L O / Sp L —
S  O  L O / L O S O / S O L p / S p L —
```

Naturally, as long as the basic isochronous units are maintained in terms of juncture and pause, the stress-pattern can be freely varied without any wrenching of the rhythm:

Lilactime   typewriter   honeysuckle   black
S O L p   / S p L O   / S O   L O / S p Pp
Black   blackbird   typewriter   black
SpPp / Sp L p /S p   LO / SpPp
Polyphonic   typewriter   honeysuckle   black
L O   S O / S p L O / S O   L O / SpPp

Whence:

scriβan   sceadugenga.   Sceotend   swaefon,
SpLp /   S O   LO /   S p L p / S p L (O) —
                      Beowulf, l. 703.
gewat   θa   ofer   waegholm   winde   gefysed
O / S O   L O / S p Lp / Sp L O / Sp L (O) —
                      Beowulf, l. 217.
Sceldes   gonnen   scanen;   scaftes   tobreken
  S O   L O / SpLp / S p L O / S p L   (O) —
            Lagamon's *Brut* (Emerson, p. 189, l. 30).
A   faire   felde   ful   of   folke   fonde   I   there   bytwene
O / S O   L O / S   O L O /   S   O L   O / SpL (O) —
            Piers Plowman, l. 17.

And:

As   kingfishers   catch   fire,   dragonflies   draw   flame
O / S p L O / S p   ⌣p / S O L p / S p L p
            Hopkins, No. 34.
As   a   dare-gale   skylark   scanted   in   a   dull   cage
O   O / Sp L p / S pLp / S O   L O / S p L —
           Hopkins, "The Caged Skylark."

The Old and Early Middle English examples were written, of course, at a time when English was still a synthetic, i.e., flexional, language. Hopkins recreates their patterns

40

because of his fondness for juxtaposed stresses and para-synthetic compounds. More recent specimens, because of the analytical tendencies and frequent monosyllabic words of modern English, have a more packed appearance.

Music of the starlight, shimmering on the sea
S O L O / S p L p / S O O L O / S
Noyes, "Haunted in Old Japan."

Dim drums throbbing in the hills half heard
S p L p / S O L O / S p L p / S
Chesterton, "Lepanto."

Sandalwood, cedarwood, and sweet white wine
S O L p / S O L O / S p L p / S
Masefield, "Cargoes."

And bonnily clinks the gold there, but drowsily blinks the eye
O / S O O L O / S p L O / S O O L O/ S
Masefield, "London Town."

The basic relation between lines in Hopkins' sprung rhythm and the "full" dipodic lines of Chesterton, Masefield, Kipling, and Noyes is obscured by Hopkins' un-cadenced handling of the dipodies SpLp, SpLO, and SpPp. The relation of sprung rhythm to the Old and Middle English alliterative "long line" is masked by his use of the dipodic measure in lines consisting of three or two measures, viz., "pentameters" of three dipodies, and "tetrameters" of two. But both relations are made certain by the metrical and personal evidence found in Hopkins' "Preface," Letters, and Notebooks.

The "Preface" unequivocally states that sprung rhythm is measured in feet of from one to four syllables, that these feet are assumed to be of equal length, that in the recommended scansion the stress falls regularly on the first syllable of each foot, and that the feet are of four possible types, "a monosyllable, the so called accentual Trochee, Dactyl, and the First Paeon." Now an unhurried first paeon (—xxx) cannot occur in English without a light stress on one of the three "unstressed" syllables; and the other facts are irreconcilable either with the essential structure of the English language or with Hopkins' poetic practice, except on the assumption that his sprung rhythm was dipodic.

The same result follows from isolated but extraordinarily significant references in the *Letters*. Thus (II. v):

. . . if the common ballad measure allows of our having (say) in a fourfoot line "Terrible butchery, frightful slaughter" why, on principle, shd. we not say "Terrible butchery, fell swoop" and that be four feet? or further why not "Sanguinary consequences, terrible butchery"?—except indeed, what of course in practice and actual versewriting is important, that *consequences* is a clumsy halting word which makes the line lag.

This reveals not only the dipodic terms in which Hopkins was thinking, but also his grave limitations as a metrist. His failure to recognize the time-marking function of secondary stress led him into insuperable difficulties. For confirmation, we need only compare his handling, or rather mishandling, of two lines by Campbell (*Letters* II. iii):

. . . if each line has three stresses or three feet it follows that some of the feet are of one syllable only. So too "*Óne, twó*, Búckle my shóe" *passim*. In Campbell you have "And their fléet alóng the *déep próudly* shóne"—"It was tén of Ápril *mórn by* the chíme" etc.

Since Hopkins intends the italicized words here to represent stressed monosyllables counted as one foot, his

42

scansion obviously fails to accord with any normal reading of the Campbell lines, as anyone familiar with "Ye Mariners of England" and "The Battle of the Baltic" will immediately recognize. But the pattern suggested by the Hopkins markings,

L O S O / L O S p / S p P p / S p P p,

is so closely integrated with the normal tune of his sprung rhythm that these Campbell quotations make a most valuable clue to its real nature. Campbell, in fact, seems to have had almost as much to do with its origin as Milton.

. The final proof that sprung and dipodic rhythm are the same comes from Hopkins' own remarks upon the history and analogues of his new rhythm. In a first explanation to Bridges (August 21, 1877, *Letters* I. xxxvii), he not only finds it in Campbell, Milton and Welsh poetry, but also in "nursery rhymes, weather saws, and Refrains." A letter to Dixon (October 5, 1878, *Letters* II. iii) again notes its connection with "the rhythm of nursery rhymes and popular jingles." In the "Preface" to his *Poems,* he describes it as the rhythm of common speech, and once again mentions its occurrence in "nursery rhymes, weather saws, and so on." By this time, however, he has also found it in *Piers Plowman,* and thinks of Greene as "the last writer who can be said to have recognized it." By October 18, 1882 (*Letters* I. xc), he is at last becoming sufficiently acquainted with Old English poetry to say that sprung rhythm "existed in full force in Anglo saxon verse, and in great beauty." These attributions of relationship are undoubtedly correct. What is more important, they prove beyond all doubt that it is the dipodic rhythm that Hopkins is trying to describe.

Our examination of Old English dipodic verse-structure (II above) has already revealed its basic affinity with sprung rhythm poems. As the articles of G. B. Stewart have conclusively shown, *Piers Plowman* is undoubtedly written in this same rhythm, though not in the "degraded and doggrel shape" which Hopkins finds there. Ever since the revolutionary articles by William Ellery Leonard in 1918 and 1920, it has been common knowledge among metrists that "nursery rhymes, weather saws, and Refrains" are written in dipodic rhythm. Thus Hopkins' statements, however limited their application to his own technical problem, undoubtedly provide a perfectly accurate derivation for his "new rhythm."

The marked examples that Hopkins provides by way of illustration could scarcely be clearer:

Márch dúst, Ápril shówers
Bríng fórth Máy flówers.
>> *Notebooks,* p. 234.
Büsk yé, büsk / ye, my bónny bónny brĬde;
Büsk yé, büsk / ye, my wĬnsome márrow.
>> *Notebooks,* p. 236.
Óne, twó, Búckle my shóe.
>> *Letters* II. iii.
What this moúntain beméneth / and this dérke dále
And this féire féld, fúl of fólk / féire I scháll ow schéwe. . . .
A lóvely ládd on leór / in línnene iclóthed.
>> *Notebooks,* p. 235.[1]

---

[1] For further examples, cf. *Letters* I. xxiv, xxv, xlv, II. xiv; *Notebooks,* pp. 236, 234–5.

SPRUNG RHYTHM

All in all, then, Hopkins' historical account of sprung rhythm as found in the "Preface," the *Letters* and the *Notebooks* leaves very little doubt about its real metrical basis. That its identity with the age-old dipodic measures of English poetry has not been widely understood is due partly to the poet's own contradictory utterances, partly to the somewhat primitive state of metrical knowledge in his own time, partly to his inherent conservatism of linear and stanzaic forms, and partly to his free, uncadenced, and unbalanced handling of the rhythm itself. His inability to recognize the time-marking role of secondary stress inevitably confused and thwarted all attempts at explanation. No one in his day could know—as few in our day know—that the oldest English poetry is written in a dipodic rhythm of regularity and strictness. But other points are even more important. Hopkins' preoccupation with such conventional forms as the sonnet and his attempts to relate a quite different type of line to the conventional alexandrine, pentameter and tetrameter resulted in forms not usually taken by dipodic verse in English. His pentameters are actually dipodic trimeters; his tetrameters, dipodic dimeters; only his alexandrine and the rhythm of his "Spelt from Sibyl's Leaves" approximate the normal length of the English dipodic long line. Finally, we must remember that Hopkins' treatment of anacrusis and his scansion of the whole poem as a run-on unit were strange novelties for readers unaccustomed to our older poetry. It is scarcely surprising that none of his friends in his own time and few of his admirers in ours could understand what he was about.

Hopkins' actual innovations in the handling of the most traditional English rhythm are few. They are confined, for the most part, to his abrupt, non-cadenced fingering of the dipodic measures SpLp, SOLp, SpLO, and SpPp, the so-called truncated dipods. These patterns occur regularly enough in modern dipodic verse, but usually in prepared positions and linked cadences:

Where the grey seas glitter and the sharp tides shift
  O   O/ S p L p /SO L O/ S p L p /S p
And the sea-folk labour and the red sails lift.
  L   O/ SpLp / S O L O/ S p L p /S
                         Chesterton, "Lepanto."
Where the old trade's plyin' and the old flag flyin'
  O   O / SpLp / S O L O / SpLp/ S O—
                        Newbolt, "Drake's Drum."
Love is in the greenwood building him a house
  S O L O / SpLp / S O LO/ SpP
Of wild rose and hawthorn and honeysuckle boughs.
  O / S p L O/ S p L O / S O L O / S
                       Noyes, "Sherwood."

Hopkins, however, does not limit these or any other measures to definite places in the line or stanza, nor does he correlate them by means of cadence and echo. His finest poems are organized in definite rhythmic sections centering around the repetition of a single dipodic type—SpLp, SOLp, SpLO, or even SOOLOO.

In "Carrion Comfort," "The Caged Skylark," and most of the poems described as "sprung" in Bridges' "Notes," the predominant dipodic type—almost a "rhythmic signature"—is SpLp:

Not, I'll not, carrion comfort, Despair, not feast on thee;
  O / S O   LO/ SpL O / S pPO / L O S
or L O / Sp LO/ SpL O / Sp L p/S O L

SPRUNG RHYTHM

Not untwist—slack they may be—these last strands of man
O O / S p L O / S p L p / S O   L O / S
In me ór, most weary, cry *I can no more.* I can; . . .
O Lp/S pP O / SpLp /SpPO/S O L O/SpP—

As a dare-gale skylark scanted in a dull cage
O O /S p L p / S p L p / S O L O / S p L p
Man's mounting spirit in his bone-house, mean-house, dwells.
S p L O / S O L O /S p L p / S p L p / S

In "Spelt from Sibyl's Leaves," Hopkins' longest and most
complicated sonnet, it is SOOLOO (⁶⁄₄ time):

Earnest, earthless, equal attuneable, vaulty, voluminous . . .
S O   L O /S O OL O O /S O O L O O /P
   stupendous
    O L O /
Evening strains to be, time's vast, womb-of-all, home-of-all,
S O O L O O / S p L p / S O O L O O
   hearse-of-all night.
    / S O O L
Her fond yellow hornlight wound to the west, her
O / S O O L O / S O O L O /
   wild hollow hoarlight hung to the height
    S O O L O / S O O L p /
Waste; her earliest stars, earl-stars, stars principal
3 p P O / S O O L p / S p L p / S p L O O /
   overbend us,
    S O L O /
Fire-featuring heaven . . . .
S p L O O / S p P—

These few examples may be sufficient to illustrate Hop-
kins' most characteristic variation—his use of the sprung
monosyllabic foot SpPp or its sub-type SpPO. Admittedly,
he employs it, at least in the "terrible" sonnets, with ad-
mirable skill. Yet his manipulation of the dominating meas-

47

ure or "rhythm signature," which is never mentioned in his own explanations of his metrics, is even more admirable. Few passages in English verse are as profoundly moving as the final lines of "Carrion Comfort" and "Sibyl's Leaves," where, after a pyrotechnic cascade of variations and cross-rhythms, the basic tunes suddenly reappear. The strange beauty of the effect compensates for all Hopkins' theoretical inconsistencies and justifies sprung rhythm as practical and successful art.

4

Charles Williams' introduction to the second edition of Hopkins' poems contains two highly significant observations:

A good deal of attention has been paid to Gerard Hopkins's prosody, to his sprung-rhythms and logaoedic, his paeons and outrides; not so much has been spent on those habits, especially alliteration, to which English verse is more accustomed. Yet the alliteration so largely present in his poems is significant. . . .

Alliteration, repetition, interior rhyme, all do the same work: first, they persuade us of the existence of a vital and surprising poetic energy; second, they suspend our attention from any rest until the whole thing, whatever it may be, is said.

Any close reader of Hopkins will be impressed by the constant recurrence of alliteration, internal rhyme, word repetition, and assonance. Together with the complex rhythmic patterns, they undoubtedly have a vital influence upon the "obscurities" of word formation and syntax for which the poet is noted. In accounting for them, however, it is not necessary to second Williams' mystical explanation; far better to return to the cool sanity of Patmore:

> The law of alliteration is the only conceivable intrinsic mode of immediately indicating the right metrical accentuation where the language consists mainly of monosyllables and the verse admits of a varying number of unemphatic syllables, before, between, and after the accented ones.
>
> "Essay on English Metrical Law," p. 252.

Dipodic rhythm, of its very nature, requires certain technical devices for indicating the position of primary, and to some extent of secondary, stresses. Conceivably, if a poet graded vocabulary according to the grammatical importance of its elements, he could write good dipodic lines without using such devices. But with English as it is, and the readers of poetry what they are, anything but the simplest of variations would be impossible. Even in non-dipodic verse, "apt alliteration's artful aid" is frequently invoked, though chiefly for ornament. In dipodic verse, alliteration is functional. It is used, as the rarer internal rhyme, word repetition, and assonance are used, to reinforce or "overstress" the strong positions in the rhythmic pattern:

I catch her *l*ittle hand as we *l*isted to the *l*ark.
> Meredith, "Love in the Valley," l. 72.

He *c*lubbed his wretched *c*ompany a *d*ozen times a *d*ay;
> Kipling, "Army Headquarters," l. 5.

Wh*i*te for bliss and bl*i*nd for s*u*n and st*u*nned for liberty.
> Chesterton, "Lepanto," l. 33.

*A*ll across the glades of fern he *ca*lls his merry men.
> Noyes, "Sherwood," l. 42.

With her pr*i*ze upon her quarter grappled t*i*ght.
> Newbolt, "San Stefano," l. 35.

49

Will you not come *home*, brother, *home* to us again?
> Masefield, "The West Wind," l. 12.

Swa navere nolde he him *s*ugge / *so*θ hu hit ferde
> Lagamon, *Brut* (Emerson, l. 7.).

Ne θurfe we us *s*pillan, gif ge *s*pedaθ to θam:
> *The Battle of Maldon*, l. 34.

> *s*y *f*ul wide *f*ah

*f*eorres *f*olclondes, θaet min *f*reond siteθ
under *st*anhliθe   *st*orme behrimed,
> *The Wife's Lament*, ll. 46–48.

Thy *w*ring-world *r*ight foot *r*ock? lay a *l*ionlimb against me? scan
> "Carrion Comfort."

As a *d*are-gale *s*kylark *s*canted in a *d*ull cage
> *M*an's *m*ounting spirit in his bone-*house*, *m*ean-*house*, dwells—
> "The Caged Skylark."

With: *O*ur evening is *o*ver us; *o*ur night / *wh*elms, *wh*elms *a*nd
will *e*nd us . . .

Where, *self*wrung, *self*strung, *sh*eathe- and *sh*elterless, / *th*oughts
against *th*oughts in *gr*oans *gr*ind.
> "Spelt from Sibyl's Leaves."

*F*all, *g*all themselves, and *g*ash *g*old-vermilion.
> "The Windhover."

There is one, yes I *h*ave one (*H*ush there!);
Only *n*ot within *s*eeing of the *s*un,
*N*ot within the *s*ing*eing* of the *s*trong *s*un,
*T*all *s*un's *t*ing*eing*, or *t*reacherous the *t*ainting
of the *e*arth's *a*ir.
> "The Leaden Echo and the Golden Echo."

All the overstressing devices illustrated depend upon
the same principle—anticipatory familiarization with cer-
tain sounds or sound combinations, so that, upon repe-
tition, the reader is induced to give them slightly more
emphasis than usual. The more complex the stress pat-
tern, the more commonly the devices occur. We need not

be surprised that Hopkins, preoccupied with stress patterns of quite unusual complexity, should make full and constant use of all of them.

In the history of poetry, of course, the functional often becomes ornamental. Undoubtedly, much of the alliteration and assonance of modern verse is ornamental. Even in the medieval literatures the functional alliteration of Old English and the Elder Edda eventually becomes a single colored strand in the highly artificial, ornamental skein of internal rhymes, end-alliterations, assonances, and light rhymes of Skaldic verse, the Irish *droighneach*, the Middle Welsh lyrics, and Lagamon's *Brut*. In two illuminating letters to Bridges, Hopkins (I. xxx, xciii) somewhat deplores what he calls the tendencies of his "salad days" and confesses his debt to Welsh poetry for "the chiming of consonants." But he quickly mastered the principle of functional overstressing. A reading of his later poems reveals how successfully he fused the various devices into what he would call the "inscape."

For the student of Hopkins' metrics, the whole question of overstressing is extremely important. We study his metrics for a practical purpose—to be able to *perform* his poems. Careful study of his alliterations, assonances, word repetitions, and internal rhymes reveals more of the organic structure to the would-be performer than all the loops, whirls and colons of MS.B. put together. For the student of Hopkins' imagery and stylistics, however, the implications of overstressing are downright revolutionary. Ever since Bridges and Patmore first read his poems, Hopkins' "obscurities" and "coinages" have roused mingled admiration, enthusiasm and derision. Almost without exception, modern critics have accepted Mr. I. A. Richards' statement that Hopkins "may be described, without opposition, as the most obscure of English verse writers" (*Dial*, September, 1926, p. 195). Equally readily, they have accepted Mr. David Daiches' perception that Hopkins was "straining after a directness beyond that allowed by the formal syntactic use of language" (in *New Literary Values*, Edinburgh, 1936, pp. 23–51). In fact, a good deal of the admiration for and imitation of Hopkins within the last two decades springs from his notorious "obscurity." Without in any sense decrying Hopkins' real poetic genius, his acute observation of natural phenomena and his demonstrated interest in linguistic problems, we can question the validity of both statements. Any poet writing the complex metrical patterns favored by Hopkins, and marking those patterns by means of the various over-stressing devices, can scarcely fail to achieve, at least in modern English, the syntactical abbreviations, the climactic appositions, the *tmesis*, the marooned prepositions, and even the original and colorful word-compounds which distinguish Hopkins' handling of vocabulary. Yet in all such points Hopkins was anticipated by those medieval poets who, like him, were strongly interested in sound pattern, rather than in the lucid communication of ideas.

As we have already seen, the chief external characteristic of Hopkins' sprung variety of dipodic rhythm is the occurrence of non-cadenced measures in the patterns SpLp, SpLO, SOLp and SpLp. The number of normal English parasynthetic compounds, particularly alliterating compounds, usable in these patterns is severely limited. Significantly enough, most of Hopkins' coinages, so much admired for their flash and compressed imagery, are compounds of the forms SpLp, SpLO and SOLp: *firefeaturing, rook-racked, wind-wandering, weed-winding, love-laced, brass-bold, foam-froth, fell-frowning, beadbonny, foam-fleece, frailest-flixed, knee-nave, foot-fretted, gaygear, girlgrace.* If the list is extended to include compounds directly influenced by neighboring alliterations, rhymes and assonances, it is practically endless: *bonehouse, mean-house; wind-beat white-beam; selfwrung, selfstrung; world's-wildfire; wiry and white-fiery and whirlwind-swiveled; down-dugged, ground-hugged gray; fresh-firecoal chestnut-falls; shivelights and shadowtackle,* etc. These are of the same coinage as the metaphorical circumlocutions, kennings, tautological compounds and periphrases of Old English poetry: *ofer bord gebraec, deofla gedraeg, goldwine gumena, banhus, hronrad, brydbur, cwealmcuma, goldgyfa, heardhycgende, foldbold, wordhord, gumdream ofgeaf, aeðeling aergod, ginfaesten gifa,* etc.—all in *Beowulf.* Moreover, the lists of alliterating words, compounds and derivatives in the *Notebooks* seem to reveal that Hopkins searched as deliberately for such expressions as any poet of the 14th Century "Alliterative Revival." Resemblances of vocabulary between Hopkins and the medieval poets are no more accidental than the resemblances in rhythm. If he and the *Beowulf* poet show marked stylistic affinities, it is because—all questions of direct influence apart—the stylistic pressures were the same for both.

Sprung rhythm, the overstressing devices and a distinctive, if obscure, vocabulary are the interlocking segments of the Hopkins problem. To write sprung rhythm, he was obliged to use alliteration, internal rhyme, assonance and word repetition. To use these devices, he needed new compounds and syntactic shortcuts. In nothing more metaphysical than this does his "breaking down of the barriers of language" consist. That he does break them down is undoubted, but surely not to attain "precision of thought" or "a directness beyond that allowed by the formal syntactic use of language." His verbal innovations exist merely to assure the precise ordering of the musical elements in his lines.

As a poet, Hopkins was a half-musician writing a poetry half-music. From the moment when he first heard the tune he calls sprung rhythm in the Milton choruses, in Campbell, in snatches of older English verse—perhaps also in Purcell's bold handling of libretti—he tried to circumvent the lack of fluidity so inherent in the rhythms of poetry as compared with the rhythms of music. Gradually, he must have realized that he had created new fetters and trammels more straitened than those he had displaced. Like Pater, he came to understand that all art strives towards the conditions of music. Like Wagner, he eventually subordinated poetical to musical composition. His death interrupted a process of artistic self-development from the neo-Keatsian tonalities of his early poems, through the half-musical sprung rhythm period, towards that complete fusion of form and substance, of matter and manner, attainable only in pure music. Significantly, his most impressive composition was a two-choir setting for an early love—Campbell's "Battle of the Baltic."

4. THE SWEET AND LOVELY LANGUAGE

By Josephine Miles

GERARD MANLEY HOPKINS WAS A CHAMPION AND GREAT master of epithet. He expected poetry, including his poetry, to catch and convey vividly what eye saw and heart felt. *Vivid* was a word he liked to use in his letters, and he used it often with *imagery*, in praise. He denied the validity of Lessing's old distinction between painting and poetry.

"Vermilion, saffron, white" is a brilliant stroke (that is a lie, so to speak, of Lessing's that pictures ought not to be painted in verse, a damned lie—so to speak). (*Dixon*, XVI)

He demanded for poetry the colorful, descriptive, elaborate, adjectival, and in this demand agreed outstandingly with Spenser, Milton, Collins and Keats.

Many who like Hopkins' poetry like to have it made up at its best of their own wishes, some Donne, some

Anglo-Saxon, some Dryden for whom Hopkins stated his admiration outright, preferably metaphysical traits wherever possible, and little of the gloss, glow and affection of the poetic lingo of Keats's century in which Hopkins lived. I suggest no alteration in these recognitions but a change in their proportion. As for the Anglo-Saxon, Terence Heywood has shown how late he came to its study (*Poetry* 54: 209–218); as for the Metaphysicals, much of what he shared with them he shared with Milton also, in a bond which he himself stressed; and as for Keats, Hopkins never did get over him. Why should he have, except for our tender sakes? The *Letters* and *Notebooks* discuss poetry in 19th Century terms, and those were Keats terms. Tennyson and Morris disappointed, Swinburne and Browning disgusted, Keats, Barnes, Dixon, sometimes the Pre-Raphaelites, pleased; but in pleasure or displeasure, this was the field of Hopkins' acquaintance and reference. And his strongest words of praise and awe, as well as some of blame, were for Milton and Keats (*Bridges* XXX, *Dixon* II).

His poetic descriptive language was the language of Milton and Keats. In large part the regular substance and pattern of his diction has not only that magnitude of idiosyncrasy which we tend immediately to recognize, but also the constancy of descriptive tradition which we tend to pass over without recognition. In Hopkins, as in any poet of whom we are fond, we are quicker to trace traits peculiar or pleasant to us than to identify the large portion of traits assumed and accepted without stress but with thorough ease by the poet. So the sheer quantity, the repeated form and function, the regular presence, of

THE SWEET AND LOVELY LANGUAGE

Hopkins' descriptive adjectives through all the variations of his poetry help clarify some of his perhaps partly unconscious assumptions as to poetic quality, and suggest his alliance to the painter poets of whom Keats is so notably one.

Hopkins' most frequent adjectives, those he used ten times or more apiece in the fourteen hundred lines which the Oxford edition presents as completed work as distinguished from fragments, are adjectives of sense and lively response. *Sweet* was his favorite, his world was *sweet:* flowers, soul, skill, heaven, earth's being, a stallion, spells, wood, scene, notes, sending, ending, air, hopes, scions, looks, landscape, reprieve, alms, gift, fires, scarless sky, and a dozen more, were sweet. A dozen more were *lovely,* and a dozen *dear:* freshness, aspens, charity, dogged man, concern, daystar, chance, father and mother, and more, *dear;* starlight, Death, Providence, weeds, fire, behaviour, woods, manly mould, Christ, dale, lads, mile, men's selves, all "Holiest, loveliest, bravest." These are terms, especially in their contexts, of aesthetic feeling and affectionate response. They serve to make abstracts more sensible and concretes more personal. They give *skill* or *reprieve* a taste and fragrance; they are friendly toward *freshness;* they love, and find love-like, *Providence* and *starlight* as well; and together they provide the constant poetic line of early poems, *Deutschland,* late great sonnets alike.

Sweet, dear and *lovely* do not bear a strict Hopkins label. They sound quite like the 19th Century and perhaps, except for *lovely,* like the sixteenth. Neither is the natural world they modify, the nouns of earth, wood, fire, sky,

57

cloud, air and aspen, in any way idiosyncratic or pe-
culiar; in fact it is the very world Ruskin writes about as
modern in *Modern Painters,* the "inscape" and "instress,"
in Hopkins' terms, of natural objects closely admired by
the devout painter's eye. Nor are soul and skill, charity
and concern, chance and death, abstractions new to the
poetic scene; they are common to many centuries and
have been sensably qualified by many. Here runs through
Hopkins' poetry the vigor of tradition in fact and epithet.

Others of his major adjectives are equally traditional.
Good and *bad* are Elizabethan and later, seemingly terms
natural for almost any poet. Weather and nature and man
himself are bad, and gift, being and beauty good, for
Hopkins. *Bright* and *dark* are, on the other hand, "Ro-
mantic" epithets, the discrimination made first with em-
phasis by Wordsworth, Keats and Shelley. For these
three, sun, moon, day, face, or glance, were obviously
bright, and thought or vision less apparently. For Hop-
kins too sun and cloud, but also wing, borough, paling,
sandal,—a more special application.

Of the other major epithets one more is Romantic: *wild*
waters, meal-drift, hoarlight, air, in Hopkins' special
stamp. Others are colors, his distinctively, *black* west and
bough, *grey* lawn and drayhorse, *blue* days, heavens,
embers, for samples. And finally, *fresh* is distinctively his,
sounding more like him even than *lovely. Fresh* crust and
youth and thought and wind and windfalls. What's fresh
seems sweet, says Hopkins, and so he adds to the poetic
vocabulary of praise.

A substantial part of the language of his poetry is, then,
language shared, and shared more with the descriptive

58

painter poets than with the metaphysicals. His dozen most frequent epithets, appearing in all a hundred and fifty times or so, bulk large and speak in rich tone, modifying a familiar nature closely perceived. In them Hopkins appears a sensitive, an enthusiastic, a properly individualistic Pre-Raphaelite participating, against his other conscience, in the tradition of Keats. So, too, less frequent adjectives represent him: *kind, fond, sheer, poor, tender, low, high, bold, proud.* These are terms of attitude and quality much more than are the *fair, good, great, new, old, true* terms of the Elizabethans and the school of Donne. From the Elizabethans Hopkins kept just those epithets which, like sweet and good, most conveyed attitude; from the 18th Century stress of Collins and Goldsmith he kept his *fond, tender* and *kind;* and his qualities of colors, of *low* and *high, dark* and *bright,* from the scenic tradition of Milton, Wordsworth and Keats, to which his own *lovely, sheer, fresh* contributed their individual version of sense and scene. Qualified by these, Hopkins' metaphysical traits, like his metrical inventions, were smoothed and controlled in the direction of descriptive value, in its inherited adjectival pattern.

By a sort of silence Hopkins helps explain the force of his inheritance in vocabulary. He expressed little formulated theory on the subject. True, he wrote of the diction of Parnassianism, he liked or disliked certain phrases, he explained some technical uses of his own, he believed that the language of poetry should be "the current language heightened" (*Bridges,* LXII); but for every merest passing reference to phrasing there are a dozen heartfelt studyings over rhythm and meter. In sound lay Hopkins' revolutionary preoccupations. In the jolt more than the sense of his speech grew his new poetic world. And message after message, note after note, puzzled over and expounded and pieced together this new world in creation. He was well enough content with vocabulary; he had all his contemporaries' ways and means in it, and did not need to raise any issues. So in the Index to the Bridges-Dixon *Letters* where there is over a column of references under *Music,* and another under *Versification,* only one or two items are to be mustered for any diction or vocabulary topic.

One item, listed under *Wordpainting* and praising the novelists of his day, puts Hopkins square, as his adjectives themselves do, in the main line of adjective masters:

Wordpainting is, in the verbal arts, the great success of our day. Every age in art has its secret and its success, where even second rate men are masters. . . . These successes are due to steady practice, to the continued action of a school: one man cannot compass them, And wordpainting is in our age a real mastery and the second rate men of this age often beat at it the first rate of past ages. And this I shall not be bullied out of. (*Bridges,* CLV)

He blamed those of his time who were too subtle for wordpainting; he praised the novelists for using it so well.

The English line of wordpainting poets began, so far as I know, with Spenser, three hundred years before. In those three centuries, four of two dozen or more outstanding poets used adjective forms excessively, at a rate of more than one per line of verse. These were Spenser, first of all, doing almost twice as much epithetizing as Donne for example, then Milton, then Collins, then Keats, with such allied poets as Pope, Gray, Wordsworth, close sec-

THE SWEET AND LOVELY LANGUAGE

onds. These epithetizing poets shared certain outstanding poetic traits; they were shy on verbs in proportion to adjectives, they were fond of participial modifiers, especially past participles, they engaged in a good deal of compounding, they liked and increased the *y* forms of adjectives, they were partial to the two-epithet line in decorative balance. They wrote one kind of poetry, and it was a kind which Hopkins accepted.

> A gentle knight was pricking on the plaine,
> Ycladd in mightie armes and silver shielde,
> Wherein old dints of deepe woundes did remaine,
> The cruell markes of many a bloody fielde. . . .

> Yet once more, O ye Laurels, and once more
> Ye Myrtles brown, with Ivy never sere,
> I come to pluck your Berries harsh and crude,
> And with forc'd fingers rude,
> Shatter your leaves before the mellowing year.

> Farewell, for clearer Ken design'd,
> The dim-discover'd Tracts of Mind:
> Truths which, from Action's Paths retir'd,
> My silent Search in vain requir'd!

> St. Agnes' Eve—Ah, bitter chill it was!
> The owl, for all his feathers, was a-cold;
> The hare limp'd trembling through the frozen grass,
> And silent was the flock in woolly fold.

> The fine delight that fathers thought; the strong
> Spur, live and lancing like the blowpipe flame,
> Breathes once and, quenchèd faster than it came,
> Leaves yet the mind a mother of immortal song.

The regular modification in these stanzas, the mightie armes and silver shielde, Myrtles brown with Ivy never sere, dim-discover'd Tracts, silent flock in woolly fold, fine delight and strong Spur, is a way of thought in poetry which is in clear contrast to the mode, for example, of Donne, of

> I wonder by my troth, what thou, and I
> Did, till we lov'd? were we not wean'd till then?
> But suck'd on countrey pleasures, childishly?
> Or snorted we in the seaven sleepers den?

Not only are there fewer adjectives in Donne's four lines; the adjectives are not wordpainting; and the sound-and-sense structure of the writing is not set up in the expectation of a regular descriptive need. I use the contrast not as random one, of course, but as representative one. Not that four lines full of adjectives are never to be found in Donne and his kind, not that the painting poets never lay down their colors to converse, but simply that generalization about the details of the two major sorts of poetry is illustrated in these selections: that the one which uses almost twice as many adjectives is the one which uses them in persistent sensory qualification, line by line.

As Hopkins participated in the adjectival mode of composition, he shared also in its major vocabulary. While the main epithets of the metaphysical poets and their inheritors in the 19th Century, like Browning whose work Hopkins disliked, were terms of standards and human relations, *bad, good, fair, great, new, old, true*, the Miltonic vocabulary was like Hopkins', sensably and emotionally descriptive. *Dear, sweet*, and *gentle, high*, and *sad, black*,

THE SWEET AND LOVELY LANGUAGE

and *deep*, are words which Spenser stressed. *Happy, high,* and *sweet*, with a good deal of *bright* and *dark*, are Milton's too. The major epithets of Collins are *deep, fair, gentle, green, sad, soft, sweet, wild;* and of Keats, *bright, fair, golden, good, great, green, high, little, old, soft, sweet.* Of Hopkins, now we may recognize, of *sweet, dear, lovely, wild, black, grey, blue, fresh, good, bad, bright, dark,* the tone is the same. Such are the great, lovingly used, and most abundantly used, adjectives of poetry of the adjective school and of its maturity at the turn into the 19th Century. Term by term can be seen the major vocabulary building, from the *high* and *deep, gentle* and *sweet* discriminations of Spenser and Milton, through Collins' strong adjectival stress and his addition of color and wildness, to the whole "school's" acceptance, in the names of Coleridge, Wordsworth, Shelley, Keats, Tennyson and Poe, of a central core of terms, the bright and dark, deep and high, sweet and wild variety.

To this school of the vitality of the sensed and visible natural world, Hopkins went, and was at home without theory. He did not write in letters, and would not have been aware, so easy was his acceptance, that of the dozen main epithets he used so much through his whole life, all but three or four he shared with certain allied predecessors, the negative *bad* with Donne and Milton, and the rest with Keats and his earlier kin. Even his own contributions in abundance and emphasis, his *fresh* and *lovely* and his color discriminations, maintained the tradition of these poetic friends. Moreover, he did not radically change the contexts of these terms. His flowers and woods, charities and concerns, in their mixture of abstracts into the scenic world, were not far from Keats's copses and roses, bequests and essences, or even from Milton's groves and converses, though Milton's world was on the whole a far more cosmically ordered one, with its vocabulary of circles, processions and realms, as Collins' too was more processional. Painting, by Hopkins' time, was still of landscape with thoughts, but of a closer and more personal scene. Wooddove, falcon, drayhorse, were distinguished, and with the classical Boreas on the one hand, the shapes and colors of leaves on the other. Indeed, the differences in what painting poets saw to paint may be noted even more clearly in their prose than in their poetry; Keats and Hopkins, like Ruskin, in the tendency of their time, found more minute natural detail to see.

There is likeness, too, in the devices by which the adjective-users record the details of their observation and response, whether cosmic or pastoral, processional or individual. Characteristic of Hopkins and of Milton, Collins and Keats, as distinguished say from Wyatt, Donne, or Pope, is strong use, up to a third of all adjective forms, of participles as adjectives. "With forc'd fingers rude," "for clearer Ken design'd," "The hare limp'd trembling," the "Spur, live and lancing" are examples. The larger portion are past forms, and they serve to catch and fix motion and quality into a more permanent state; they work then in a way counter to action and motion in poetry, though they make use of action and motion. Where Hopkins is short on straight active verb forms, despite the general impression of many readers, he is long on these crystallizing elements. Of the most vigorous of the present forms (and his *hurling, riding, heaving, calling, swirling, poising, rolling, racing, wrestling, echoing, soaring,* are assuredly more lively than Keats's *glowing, breathing, dreaming, dying, aching, blazing, wand'ring, whisp'ring,* for example, though the two share visual terms like *dazzling*) even the most active participles are yet more statements of quality than of action.

The past forms are intensely qualitative. Few are common or repeated. The familiar *dead* of most poets is rare in Hopkins. *Laced, hung, lost, fallen, wept,* are repeated a few times. But a great amount of invention and compounding comes for Hopkins in these forms, just as it did for Milton, Collins and Keats. Keats had doubled Collins' compound epithets; Hopkins in turn doubled Keats's. His inventiveness worked here again in the main line which the adjectival poets had established. Keats's *carved, wing'd, hid, faded, unseen, moss'd,* became Hopkins' *carved, winged, dogged, cursed, freckled, fetched, plumed,* in all a somewhat rarer lot; and Keats's *eager-eyed, hot-blooded, half-anguished, deep delved, purple-stained, wild-ridged,* became Hopkins' more complicated and special *carrier-witted, scroll-leaved, whirl wind-swivelled, else-minded, heart-forsook, care-coiled, bell-swarmed, dapple-dawn-drawn, no-man-fathomed, five-lived, rarest-veined.* The change is not one, as far as I can see, toward greater metaphysical farfetchedness but rather is an intensification of quality statement, an emphasis on the special perceivable nature of things, the physical sense of whirlwind, leaf, care, bell qualities. Emphasis is just what Hopkins said, in his early essay on "Poetic Diction," the accented past participle is good for. Poetry needs more emphasis of all sorts he said there, more 18th Century liveliness, more

19th Century vividness to make mere flat "Parnassian" descriptiveness come alive. The accented past participle does have a life-giving quality when chosen thus in substitute for adjective, rather than for verb; the very choice shows the direction from which Hopkins felt himself to be working.

"O well wept" should be written asunder, not "wellwept." It means "you do well to weep" and is framed like "well caught" or "well run" at a cricketmatch (*Bridges*, XLI).

Here is the life in the structure for Hopkins, and a life from spoken language it is. But a little later, writing on the need for reshaping English compounds to poetic use, Hopkins contrasted *potato* as an ugly and laughable word to *earthapple* as a stately one (*Bridges*, XCIV). This is the life in the sense-stress for Hopkins; the compound can give the fuller sense quality, the rhetorical "colors" of the thing, as Aristotle had long recommended and as Spenser, Milton, Shelley and Keats had mainly contrived in English poetry to show.

The *flint-flake, white-fiery, lovely-dumb, piece-bright, lull-off, silk-sack, very-violet-sweet,* and later more infrequent *wet-fresh, age-old, rope-over* epithetical compounds without verb forms, which amount to nearly half the number, bear out Hopkins' need to specify quality as closely as hyphens could. Adjective or adverb plus noun or adjective do the attributing. From the thing its quality is drawn by punctuation, as if there in the making. So most commonly the meaning of *with* or *like* is assumed in the participle forms, in *crimson-cresseted* or *bleak-leaved* for example.

So also the *y* forms of the adjective, characteristic of the painter poets, gave Hopkins great scope in quality-making, by condensing and assuming *like*. He used more of these forms than any poet I know; not only the *starry, mazy, airy, glassy, watery, wintry, vaulty, wiry,* familiar from Keats and the 18th Century, but the *roundy, branchy, beadbonny, fretty, barrowy* which sound less familiar. His word-making force was a force toward analogy and especially sense analogy, thereby to catch the inner landscape in the outer. His prose epitheting worked the same way. "I am, so far as I know, permanently here, but permanence with us is ginger-bread permanence; cobweb, soapsud, and frost-feather permanence" (*Bridges,* XLIII). This is far from the metaphysical searching of microcosmic relationships; it is the crumbling, spattering, and weighing of the feeling. "Feathery rows of young corn," wrote Hopkins as a note to himself (*Notebooks,* p. 41). "Ruddy, furred and branchy tops of the elms backed by rolling cloud." And of a sunset: "Above the green in turn appeared a red glow, broader and burlier in make; it was softly brindled, and in the ribs or bars the color was rosier, in the channels where the blue of the sky shone through it was a mallow colour" (*Dixon,* App. II). Hopkins, like Ruskin, was a notebook sketcher and painter, by nature as by convention a wordpainter. When he was in a hurry and had little to say of the day which was closing, if it were fine he often wrote *Fine* in his Journal, but often *Bright*.

The terms and devices of the painting poets were satisfying then to Hopkins, satisfying at least as we see satisfaction in constant use and agreement, be it in explicit defense or only in taking for granted. The epithets and forms most often recurring, in poem after poem, early and late, are the epithets and forms of Keats and his line, the words of thought in scene, the relatively few active verbs and negatives and small undecorative conversational words, the discriminating compounds and the crystallizing participles, the catching and rendering the qualities of things, the vivid images. "I want Harry Ploughman to be a vivid figure before the mind's eye; if he is not that the sonnet fails" (*Bridges,* CLV).

One would quickly say that Hopkins' poetry is much more than these matters of modification, and I should agree, but as it is more, it is also these. These he did not puzzle over, but these were the assumptions past which his puzzles, of meter, of grammatical compression and lyrical intensity, went. In every poem simple descriptiveness in 19th Century terms underlay the complexities, as in "To what serves Mortal Beauty?" the *flung, prouder form, lovely lads, wet-fresh windfalls, swarmed Rome, dear chance, barren stone, love's worthiest, World's loveliest, sweet gift, better beauty,* underlay in all confidence of accepted poetical substance the packed accents, broken rhyme-words, repetitions and ellipses, and gnomic meanings.

To what serves mortal beauty—dangerous; does set dancing blood—the O seal-that-so feature, flung prouder form
Than Purcell tune lets tread to? See: it does this: keeps warm

Men's wits to the things that are; what good means—where a glance
Master more may than gaze, gaze out of countenance.
Those lovely lads once, wet-fresh windfalls of war's storm,

THE SWEET AND LOVELY LANGUAGE

How then should Gregory, a father, have gleaned else from swarm-
ed Rome? But God to a nation dealt that day's dear chance.

To man, that needs would worship block or barren stone,
Our law says: Love what are love's worthiest, were all known;
World's loveliest—men's selves. Self flashes off frame and face.
What do then? how meet beauty? Merely meet it; own
Home at heart, heaven's sweet gift; then leave, let that alone.
Yea, wish that though, wish all, God's better beauty, grace.

Here, far less obviously than in "The dappled die-away
Cheek and wimpled lip, The gold-wisp, the airy-grey
Eye, all in fellowship" sort of poem, but still with ap-
parent force, the adjectival descriptive standards work
and persist.

It takes a whole poem to convey Hopkins' individual na-
ture, because it is the dynamics that is his. Cut crosswise,
as by an index of first lines, the poetry immediately shows
its alliances as strongly as its special traits. In the long-
est group, under *T*, simple statement works most often
with the regular descriptive epithets, *best* and *bare, fine*
and *fresh* and *massy, strong* and *darksome;* and the par-
ticiples.

The best ideal is the true
The boughs, the boughs are bare enough
'The child is father to the man'
The dappled die-away
Thee, God, I come from, to thee go
The Eurydice—it concerned thee, O Lord
The fine delight that fathers thought; the strong
The furl of fresh-leaved dogrose down
There is a massy pile above the waste
'The Rose is a mystery'—where is it found?

69

The sea took pity: it interposed with doom
The shepherd's brow, fronting forked lightening, owns
The times are nightfall, look, their light grows less;
The world is charged with the grandeur of God.
This darksome burn, horseback brown,
Thou are indeed just, Lord, if I contend
Though no high-hung bells or din
Thou mastering me
Thou that on sin's wages starvest,
To him who ever thought with love of me
Tom—garlanded with squat and surly steel
To whom the stranger lies my lot, my life
Towery city and branchy between towers;
To what serves mortal beauty—dangerous; does set danc-

Some of the most eccentric single lines, ones that leap out as Hopkins, are ones that spring from adjective center: "Cloud-puffball, torn tufts, tossed pillows flaunt forth, then chevy on an air," "Earth, sweet Earth, sweet landscape with leaves throng," "Earnest, earthless, equal, attuneable, vaulty, voluminous, . . . stupendous," "Hard as hurdle arms, with a broth of goldish flue," "Have fair fallen, O fair, fair have fallen, so dear," "Wild air, world-mothering air."

What Hopkins' inventive rhetoric of structure did for his rich epithet substance was to richen it further. His *sweet, lovely, dear, wild, fresh, good, bad, black* and *grey, bright* and *dark*, he exaggerated and specialized in the ways they had already been exaggerated and specialized but more so: by repetition and exclamation, by compounding and the piling up of vigorous participial modification, by color, variety, and affectionately detailed application. What Lionel Trilling described as opposed by Matthew Arnold in his era (*Arnold,* p. 149), Hopkins maintained: intense piety, rushing to meet life, violence of imagery, multitudinousness. The language of this intensity Hopkins did not have to invent; as a reader he had learned and liked it; he had simply to elaborate and to use it. The vocabulary and technique of epithet which he shared with Milton, Keats and the painter poets made him see afresh, and then were lent to a deeper hearing afresh.

What I have noted here about Hopkins' language is counter to the warnings of F. R. Leavis, that "Hopkins belongs with Shakespeare, Donne, Eliot and the later Yeats as opposed to Spenser, Milton and Tennyson" (*New Bearings,* p. 171); of Terence Heywood, that "Critics have fortunately given up likening Hopkins to Milton," because he "is *not* in the Spenser-Milton-Tennyson tradition" (*Poetry,* 54:271-9); and of E. E. Phare, that "His likeness to Keats is largely potential and a matter of conjecture" (p. 41). Certainly these warnings are wise if one is to look for the lone master in Hopkins. But he himself was devoted to schools and to schooling, the successes "due to steady practice, to the continued action of a school: one man cannot compass them." When he described the Romantic and the Lake schools he wrote to Dixon (XXII), "I suppose the same models, the same masters, the same tastes, the same keepings, above all, make the school." In respect to tastes and masters the epithet keepings of Hopkins should well, I think, be considered; for the master is great in his school.

5. INSTRESS OF INSCAPE

By Austin Warren

THE EARLY HOPKINS FOLLOWS KEATS AND THE "MEDIEVAL school" (as he called the Pre-Raphaelites). The latest Hopkins, who wrote the sonnets of desolation, was a poet of tense, economic austerity. Their nearest parallel I can call would be Donne's "holy sonnets": "Batter my heart" and "If poisonous minerals." For mode in "Andromeda" and the later sonnets (1885–9), Hopkins himself projected "a more Miltonic plainness and severity": he is thinking of Milton's sonnets and the choruses of *Samson*. In 1887 he invoked another name: "my style tends always more towards Dryden."

The middle period, which opens with the "Wreck of the Deutschland" (1885) and closes with "Tom's Garland" and "Harry Ploughman," both written in 1885, is the period of experiment. But it is also the most Hopkinsian,— the most markedly and specially his.

Middle Hopkins startles us by its dense rich world, its crowded Ark, its plentitude and its tangibility, its particularity of thing and word. There is detailed precision of image ("rose moles all in stipple upon trout that swim"). The poet is enamored of the unique, the "abrupt self."

The exploration of Middle Hopkins,—its style, the view of life and art implicit in its style,—may well start from the institutions and movements from which the poet learned, in which he participated. The motifs are the Ritualist Movement, Pre-Raphaelitism, Aestheticism, linguistic renovation, England, the Catholic Church. In Hopkins' celebration of the sensuous, the concrete, the particular—his "instress of the inscapes"—all of these converge.

As a Catholic, Hopkins was an incarnationist and a sacramentalist: the sacraments are the extensions of the Incarnation. As a Catholic, he believed that man is a compound of matter and form, and that his body, resurrected, will express and implement his soul through all eternity. "Man's spirit will be flesh-bound when found at best, But unencumbered. . . ." Like all Catholic philosophers, he believed in an outer world independent of man's knowing mind—he was, in the present sense of the word, a "realist."

Hopkins was an Englishman, of a proud and patriotic sort. This is not always remembered, partly because he became the priest of a Church viewed by his compatriots as Continental, or Italian, or international. But there is an English way of being Catholic.[1] Hopkins was not an "old

[1] Cf. The English Way: *Studies in English Sanctity from St. Bede to Newman* (ed. M. Ward, 1933) and the studies of Dom Augustine Baker, Lingard, and Hopkins—by Fr. D'Arcy—in *Great Catholics* (ed. C. Williamson, 1939).

Catholic" of the sturdy, unemotional variety nourished on Challoner's *Garden of the Soul;* no convert could be that. But, like his admired Newman, and unlike Manning and Faber (also converts), he was "Gallican" not Ultramontane, British not Italian in his devotional life and rhetoric. He remembers when England was Catholic, when the pilgrims frequented the shrine of our Lady of Walsingham.

> Deeply surely, I need to deplore it,
> Wondering why my master bore it,
> The riving off that race
> So at home, time was, to his truth and grace
>
> That a starlight-wender of ours would say
> The marvelous Milk was Walsingham Way
>   And one—but let be, let be;
> More, more than was will yet be.

The four real shapers of Hopkins' mind were all Britons; we might go further and say, all were British empiricists—all concerned with defending the ordinary man's belief in the reality and knowability of things and persons.

Two of them were encountered at Oxford. Pater, who remained his friend, was one of his tutors. In the abstractionist academic world, Pater boldly defended the concrete—of the vital arts and music of perception, of the unique experience. "Every moment some form grows perfect in hand or face, some tone on the hills or the sea is choicer than the rest. . . ." Though Hopkins could not conceivably have written so representatively, abstractly ". . . hills . . . sea . . . choicer," the text pleads for a stressing of the inscapes. Hopkins followed some lectures by Pater on Greek philosophy: perhaps he heard, in an

74

earlier version, Pater's lectures on Plato and Platonism, in which, with monstrous effrontery, the Doctrine of Ideas was praised as giving contextual interest to the concrete.

With Ruskin, whose *Modern Painters* he read early and admiringly, Hopkins shared the revolt against that neo-classical grandeur of generality praised by Johnson and expounded by Reynolds. The influence of Ruskin—art medievalist, devout student of clouds, mountains, trees—is pervasive in Hopkins' sketches (five of which are reproduced in the *Note-Books*) and in his journalizing—his meticulously technical descriptions of church architecture (often neo-Gothic) and scenery.

Hopkins follows the general line of Ruskin in more than art. Remote from him is the old "natural theology" which finds the humanly satisfactory and well furnished world such an effect of its Creator as the watch of the watch-maker. Nor does he, after the fashion of some mystics and Alexandrians, dissolve Nature into a system of symbols translating the real world of the spirit. Like Ruskin, he was able to recover the medieval and Franciscan joy in God's creation. And like Ruskin he protested against an England which is "seared with trade . . . and wears man's smudge." His political economy, as well as it can be construed, was Ruskinian; what may be called Tory Socialist or Distributist.

It was to Newman, his great predecessor, that Hopkins wrote when he decided to become a Roman Catholic. And Newman's closest approach to a philosophical work, his *Grammar of Assent* (1870), interested Hopkins so far that in 1883 he planned to publish (should Newman agree) a commentary on it. There were marked temperamental

75

and intellectual differences between the men. Newman, much the more complex and psychologically subtle, could feel his way into other men's minds as Hopkins could not. Hopkins was the closer dialectician and scholar. He did not share Newman's distrust of metaphysics, including the scholastic, his tendency to fideism; but he was, like Newman (in words the latter used of Hurrell Froude), "an Englishman to the backbone in his severe adherence to the real and the concrete."

The great medieval thinker who most swayed Hopkins' spirit to peace, Duns Scotus, was also a Briton, had been an Oxford professor. He was "Of reality the rarest-veinéd unraveler": he was able to analyze, disengage from the complex in which they appear, the thinnest, most delicate strands ("vein" may be either anatomical or geological). Perhaps "rarest-veinéd unraveler" is a kind of *kenning* for the philosopher's epithet, the Subtle Doctor. Scotus, the Franciscan critic of the Dominican Thomas Aquinas, was centrally dear to Hopkins by virtue of his philosophical validation of the individual. St. Thomas held that, in the relation of the individual to his species, the "matter" individuates, while the "form" is generic: that is, that the individuals of a species reproductively multiply their common originative pattern. Scotus insisted that each individual has a distinctive "form" as well: a *haecceitas,* or thisness, as well as a generic *quidditas,* or whatness.

After meeting with this medieval Franciscan, Hopkins, taking in "any inscape of sky or sea," thought of Scotus. The word, of Hopkins' coinage, occurs already in his Oxford note-books. Suggested presumably by "landscape": an "inscape" is any kind of formed or focussed view, any pattern discerned in the natural world. Being so central a word in his vocabulary and motif in his mental life, it moves through some range of meaning: from sense-perceived pattern to inner form. The prefix seems to imply a contrary, an outer-scape—as if to say that an "inscape" is not mechanically or inertly present, but requires personal action, attention, a seeing and *seeing into*.

The earliest "Notes for Poetry" cite "Feathery rows of young corn. Ruddy, furred and branchy tops of the elms backed by rolling clouds." "A beautiful instance of inscape *sided* on the *slide*, that is successive sidings on one inscape, is seen in the behavior of the flag flower. . . ." In 1873, two years before the "Deutschland," he "Saw a shoal of salmon in the river and many hares on the open hills. Under a stone hedge was a dying ram: there ran slowly from his nostrils a thick flesh-coloured ooze, scarlet in places, coiling and roping its way down so thick that it looked like fat."

He made notes on ancient musical instruments and on gems and their colors: "beryl—watery green; carnelian—strong flesh red, Indian red. . . ." His love of precise visual observation never lapsed. Nor did his taste for research. Like Gray, he had a scholarly, fussy antiquarianism, adaptable to botany or archaeology. He liked "Notes and Queries," details, studies in place-names, amateur etymologies.

What is perhaps his most brilliant prose celebrates the self and its wonders: "That taste of myself, of I and me above and in all things, which is more distinctive than the taste of ale or alum. . . ." Other selves were mysterious. As a shy man, he found it easier to reach natural "inscapes" than to know other selves. He hadn't Newman's psychological finesse; wrote no psychic portraits matching by their sharpness and delicacy his notations of ash-trees. The men in his poems are seen as from a distance—sympathetically but generically.

But he gloried in the range and repertory of mankind. Like Chesterton, who was concerned that, in lying down with the lamb, the lion should "still retain his royal ferocity," Hopkins wanted monks to be mild and soldiers to be pugnacious. He imagined Christ incarnate again as a soldier. He didn't want other men to be like himself—scholarly, aesthetic, neurotic: he was drawn to soldiers, miners, Felix Randall the Blacksmith and Harry the Ploughman, to the rough and manly manual laborers. And each of these selves he wished to be functioning not only characteristically but intensely, violently, dangerously—on their mettle, like the Windhover, like Harry Ploughman, like the "Eurydice's" sailor who, "strung by duty, is strained to beauty. . . ."

In poetry, he desired both to record inscapes and to use words so that they would exist as objects. His was a double particularity.

Poetry, he wrote, shortly before the "Deutschland," is "speech framed to be heard for its own sake and interest even over and above its interest of meaning. Some [subject] matter and meaning is essential to it but only as an element necessary to support and employ the shape which is contemplated for its own sake. Poetry is in fact speech for the inscape's sake—and therefore the inscape must be dwelt on."

In 1862, he was already collecting words—particularistic, concrete words. The earliest entries in the *Note-Books* are gritty, harshly tangy words, "running the letter," "grind, gride, grid, grit, groat, grate . . ." and "crock, crank, kranke, crick, cranky. . . ." He is also aroused by dialectal equivalents which he encounters: *whisket* for *basket*, *grindlestone* for *grindstone*. He notes linguistic habits: an observed laborer, when he began to speak "quickly and descriptively, . . . dropped or slurred the article." He attends to, and tries to define, the sundry schools of Latin pronunciation—this while the priests say mass. He inquires concerning the character of the Maltese language; wants to learn Welsh—not primarily in order to convert the local Wesleyans back to their ancestral faith.

As a beginning poet, Hopkins followed Keats and the "medieval school." Even in his middle style, there remain vestiges of the earlier decorative diction, frequent use of "beauty," "lovely," "dear," "sweet" ("that sweet's sweeter ending"). But already in 1866, "The Habit of Perfection," though dominantly "medieval," anticipates the later mode:

> This ruck and reel which you remark
> Coils, keeps, and teases simple sight.

"The Wreck of the Deutschland" (1875) inaugurates Hopkins' middle period (his first proper mastery). The diction is as remarkable as the rhythm. Characteristic are homely dialectal words, words which sound like survivors from Anglo-Saxon, and compound epithets. From the concluding stanzas of the "Deutschland" come these lines:

> Mid-numbered He in three of the thunder-throne!
> Not a dooms-day dazzle in his coming nor dark as he came;

and

> Dame, at our door
> Drowned, and among our shoals,
> Remember us in the roads, the heaven-haven of the
> Reward: . . .

From "The Bugler's First Communion":

> Forth Christ from cupboard fetched, how fain I of feet
> To his youngster take his treat!
> Low-latched in leaf-light housel his too huge godhead.

Modern readers take it for granted that Hopkins was influenced by Old English poetry. In his excellent *New Poets from Old: A Study in Literary Genetics,* Henry Wells notes that all the technical features representative of that poetry appear conspicuously in Hopkins; judges him far nearer to Cynewulf than to Chaucer; finds a plausible parallel to a passage in *Beowulf.* But by his own statement, Hopkins did not learn Anglo-Saxon till 1882, and seems never to have read either *Beowulf* or Cynewulf. There need of course be no pedantic mystery here. Hopkins knew something of *Piers Plowman* and is likely to have known some specimens of Old English versification.

In any case, Hopkins was already a student of Welsh poetry and an attentive reader of linguistic monographs; and he belongs among the poets who can be incited to poetry by scholars' prose.

In 1873–4, he taught "rhetoric" at Manresa House, wrote the observations on that subject collected in the *Note-Books.* His notes lead us to the *Lectures on the English Language,* published in 1859 by the versatile American scholar, George P. Marsh. This book is full of matter calculated to excite a poet, for Marsh has a real interest in the future (as well as the past) of the language and a real interest in the literary (as well as the pragmatic) use of words. The whole direction of his book suggests that literary experiment can find much in its purpose in literary history, that new poetry can come from old. Ending his lecture on "Accentuation and Double Rhymes," he urges: "We must enlarge our stock [of rhyming words] by the revival of obsolete words and inflections from native sources," or introduce substitutes for rhyme; in the following, the 25th Chapter, he incitingly discusses alliteration (with illustrations from *Piers Plowman*), consonance—e.g., "bad, led"; "find, band" (with illustrations from Icelandic poetry and invented English examples), and assonance (with illustrations from the Spanish). Hopkins' quotations from *Piers* are Marsh's; only in 1882 did he study *Piers*, and then without admiration, regarding its verse as a "degraded and doggrel" form of Anglo-Saxon sprung rhythm.

To both Bridges and Dixon, curious concerning the new poetic method of the "Deutschland," Hopkins says nothing of Old English nor of *Piers Plowman* but speaks of nursery rhymes, the choruses of *Samson*, and of his reading in Welsh poetry (which he began studying in 1875). "The chiming of the consonants I got in part from the Welsh, which is very rich in sound and imagery." H. I. Bell, a recent student of Welsh poetry, distinguishes four types of *cynghanedd*—two offering consonantal sequences (like "Night may dare / not my dearest"), another with a pattern of internal rhyme ("If to the grove she roveth"), and a fourth combining internal rhyme and alliteration ("Dais*es bl*oom, and ros*es bl*ow"). Traits common to Old English and Middle Hopkins (scant use of articles, prepositions and pronouns; constant use of compound words) are shared by both with Welsh poetry.

Then there is a third line for Hopkins' diction. He derives, through Barnes and Furnivall at least, from an imprecisely defined group of historians and philologists who may be called Teutonizers and who challenged the dominance of the Latin and Romance—the "civilized," learned, and abstract elements in our language. These linguistic protestants were motivated by nationalist or regionalist feeling or by anti-intellectualism or both.

One of these protestants was the Oxford historian, E. A. Freeman, who chronicled the Norman Conquest and himself resisted it. As early as 1846, he was praising the Teutonic part of our language as affording "expression mostly of greater strength than their romance synonyms for all purposes of general literature"; and he used the phrase "pure English" for a diction purged of these synonyms. Later, he purged and prodded. In 1872 he writes to a disciple on style: "Don't be afraid . . . I find that fifteen or sixteen years back, I talked of 'commencement,' 'conclusion,' and 'termination.' I really believe that, in these times, simplicity of style comes only by long practice." Another Anglicizer was F. J. Furnivall, a founder, in 1864, of the Early English Text Society, and a constant editor of texts, for which he wrote Forewords (not prefaces) and Afterwords. He began his intellectual career under the influence of Ruskin and Maurice, was active in the Working Men's College, and protested that his interest in early literature was not linguistic but social.

Another founder of the EETS, R. C. Trench, published in 1855 his engaging *English, Past and Present*. The second lecture considers "English as it might have been" had the Normans not invaded. Admitting that there have been gains in the mixture of linguistic stocks, Trench is concerned with defining the losses. He argues that, while our present cerebral and technical words derive from the classical languages, the Anglo-Saxon might have developed—chiefly by compounding, as German has done—such a vocabulary. Even *impenetrability* could have been matched, by *unthoroughfaresomeness*, an ungraceful word but an accurate equivalent. Theological language would be intelligible to farmhand as well as scholar if we said *again-buying* for *redemption*, *middler* for *mediator*, "Christ fellow-feels for His people" instead of "He sympathizes."

In the tradition of Trench, but much more violent, William Barnes lamented the linguistic Conquest of English and declared the old stock still capable of extension by compounding. Instead of *photograph*, we should say *sunprint* or *flameprint*. Indeed, all our current Latinisms we should replace out of the "wordstores of the landfolk." Barnes's nominations are all flavorsome; samples are *wordrich* (copious of speech), *overyearn* (commiserate), *gleecraft* (music), *outclear* (elucidate), *faithheat* (enthusiasm), *footkeys* (pedals), *withwrinkling* (spiral), *sleepstow* (dormitory), and *craftly* (technical). He regretted the loss of *inwit* in place of *conscience;* and to serve instead of *subjective* and *objective* (those psychological-philosophical terms which Coleridge introduced from Germany) he suggested *inwoning* and *outwoning*.

83

Barnes had something of a following among literary people; was publicly praised by Patmore, Gosse, Bridges, Hardy. His poetry, early read, Hopkins preferred to Burns's—liked its "West country instress"; but he learned most from the prose. Barnes's *Speechcraft* [i.e., Grammar], says Hopkins in 1882, is "written in an unknown tongue, a soul of modern Anglosaxon, beyond all that Furnival in his wildest Forewords ever dreamed. . . . [Evidently Hopkins was familiar with the publications of the Early English Text Society.] It makes one weep to think what English might have been, for in spite of all that Shakespeare and Milton have done with the compound ["impure" English] I cannot doubt that no beauty in a language can make up for want of purity. In fact, I am learning Anglosaxon and it is a vastly superior thing to what we have." He cites Barnes's wondrous "pitches of suchness" (for "degrees of comparison"): "We *ought* to call them so, but alas!" [2]

Hopkins' characteristic critical and philosophical terminology follows closely the counsel of Trench and Barnes: that is, it is a compounding of Old English roots and suffixes to suit new needs and to replace Latinic terms. *Inwit* (for *conscience*) and Barnes's *inwoning* (*subjective*) sug-

---

[2] *Arabia Deserta* (1888) was written partly, says Doughty, to show "my dislike of the Victorian English." In order to show there was an alternative, he devised an idiom making large use of pre-Miltonic words (after the model of Old English, Trench, and Barnes). "Doughty's English" is the subject of a Society for Pure English Tract (no. 51, 1939). Bridges admired Doughty's work; Hopkins, who did not, but who knew it only in excerpts, took the view that all archaism is an affectation and hence bad.

gest *instress* and *inscape*. Hopkins explains his special use of *sake* (the being a thing has outside itself) by analytic parallel of the compounds *forsake, namesake, keepsake.* The terminology of the *Comments on the Spiritual Exercises* (1880) is particularly Hopkinsian (e.g., *pitch, stress, burl*). Says Pick, "He uses almost a new language and doesn't provide a dictionary." To Bridges, Hopkins wrote of his manuscript book on rhythm, "It is full of new words, without which there can be no new science."

His doctrine of the language for poetry, nowhere exposited, was assuredly different. Archaism—the use of obsolete words for literary effect—he repudiated. His oddities (like "pashed," "fashed," "tucked," "degged") are generally dialectal; and it is safe to assume that his words of Old English lineage were collected and used by him as dialectal, still spoken, English: not "inkhorn" terms but folkspeech. Even when he thought he was improvising he was—at least in one instance—remembering: his alleged coinage, "louched" (slouched, slouching), was, as Bridges observed, to be found in Wright's Dialect Dictionary.

Whenever Hopkins explains his words (as he stands always ready to do to his friends), the particularity of the words, their compactness and detail, is made manifest. "Stickles—Devonshire for the foamy tongues of water below falls."

He defends "bole" thus: "It is not only used by poets but seems technical and *proper* [i.e., exactly belonging to] and in the mouth of timber merchants and so forth." Of "flit," called into question by a correspondent, he writes:

85

"I myself always use it and commonly hear it used among our people. I think it is at least a North Country word, used in Lancashire, for instance. . . ."

His compoundings are another matter. Though analogues can be offered from Browning, Hopkins came to them (I suppose) by way of medieval poetry, English and Welsh, and by way of Marsh, Trench and Barnes. Here the vindication would be that to compound freely was to restore to the English language that power it once had possessed: the words compounded, or the root and suffix or prefix, were separately familiar and oral. He writes "spendsavour salt" (the salt which is spending its savour and on its way to being the Biblical salt which has lost its savour), *bloomfall, trambeam, backwheels,* "Though worlds of *wanwood* [dark or pale trees] *leafmeal* [cf. "piecemeal": the suffix means "by bits," "by portions"] lie."

Judged by its effect and its internal intent, Hopkins' poetry finds partial parallels in Holst, Delius and Vaughan Williams. As (without the precise imitation of Warlock or the archaism of Dolmetsch) they sought to resume "English" music where its genuine succession was interrupted, at the Restoration, and to go creatively back to the English glory of folksong, madrigal, the modes, to Dowland, Bull and Byrd—so Hopkins seems to be reaching back, while he reached forward, to an "English" poetry. Probably we may add, to an English Catholic poetry; and suppose that his pushing back of the Elizabethans had some incentive in his desire to get back of the Reformation to the day when all England was at once Catholic and English.

86

Like the poetry of the bards and the scops, Hopkins' poetry was to be oral but not conversational, formal and rhetorical without being bookish. It used dialectal words without attempting, like Barnes's *Poems of Rural Life,* to be local and homely; it uses folk-words in "serious" poetry. Hopkins' poems intend, ideally, an audience never actually extant, composed of literarily alert countrymen and linguistically adept, folk-concerned scholars; he had to create by artifice what his poetry assumed as convention. "The Wreck" and "Tom's Garland" suggest, adumbrate, a greater poetry than they achieve.

To create an English and Catholic convention of poetry and poetic language: this was too grand an order for one Victorian poet. The experiments are yet more important than the achievement; the comparative failures more interesting than the good whole poems.

The ideal of poetry must be to instress the inscapes without splintering the fabric of the universe, and, expressionally, to make every word rich in a way compatible with the more than additively rich inclusive structure of the whole poem.

In Hopkins' poems, the word, the phrase, the local excitement, often pulls us away from the poem. And in the more ambitious pieces, the odes as we may call them ("The Wreck," "Spelt from Sibyl's Leaves," "Nature is a Heraclitean Fire"), there is felt a discrepancy between texture and structure: the copious, violent detail is matched by no corresponding mythic or intellectual vigor. Indeed, both the Wrecks are "occasional," commissioned pieces which Hopkins works at devotedly and craftfully, as Dryden did at his *Annus Mirabilis,* but which, like Dry-

87

den's poem, fail to be organisms. Hopkins wasn't a story-teller, and he was unable to turn his wrecks into myths of Wreck: they remain historical events enveloped in meditations. "The Bugler-Boy" and other poems suffer from the gap between the psychological *naïveté* and the purely literary richness. To try prose paraphrases of the middle poems is invariably to show how thin the thinking is. Hopkins' mind was first aesthetic, then technical: he thought closely on metaphysical and prosodic matters: his thinking about beauty, man and Nature is unimpressive.

The meaning of the poems hovers closely over the text, the linguistic surface of the poems. The rewarding experience of concern with them is to be let more and more into words and their linkages, to become absorbed with the proto-poetry of derivation and metaphorical expansion, to stress the inscapes of our own language.

6. HOPKINS' SANCTITY

By Robert Lowell

WHAT NONE OF THE FOUR PREVIOUS WRITERS HAS STRESSED sufficiently and what is difficult to put objectively and with relevance is the heroic sanctity of Hopkins' life. His inebriating exuberance: the experiments in meter and language, the sketches, the novel musical compositions, the curiously particular and charged observations on nature and the critical obiter dicta, the proposed introductory book to science, the proposed critical edition of Newman's *Grammar of Assent,* the designing a flask for Bridges; all this is balanced by the strict fastidiousness of his religious life, a fastidiousness which, had there been nothing else to Hopkins, might have brought him a sort of small and humorous fame as the absurd Jesuit. The life, of course, has its analogy in the poetry, in what might be called the éclat of his utterance and technique. Both were so superior and so original that few readers in his lifetime could

89

follow. In almost anyone else this swirl of diversities would have been ruinous, but in Hopkins there was achievement. His daring is sober, his obedience is alive.

Hopkins' sanctity—he would have been a saint had he written nothing—was much more. Mr. John Pick in a recent book has shown to what an extent Hopkins' life is based on the exercises of St. Ignatius. I shan't try to specify just what a Jesuit's life is—a soldier's life, close to the physical Incarnation, in some ways rather footloose; it seems to flower most in furious activity, as in the case of the Canadian martyrs. Hopkins' life was short and broken. But like Luigi Gonzaga's it is a complete Christian life and it ended with conquest.

Like other practiced writers, Hopkins was able to use most of his interests and experiences in his poetry. However, if we compare him with his peers in the 18th and 19th Centuries, we see that he was able to do this rather more than the others. Why? This is where the problem of sanctity is relevant. When we examine Pope, Wordsworth, Coleridge, Arnold, or Browning, I think we realize that after a certain point all these men—all of them great writers at times and highly religious in their fashion— stopped living; they began to reflect, to imagine, to moralize: some single faculty kept on moving and fanning the air, but the whole-man had stopped. Consequently, in their writings they mused, they fabled, they preached, they schemed and they damned. Hopkins is substantially dramatic (*in act* according to the language of scholastic philosophy).

Now to be thoroughly *in act* is human perfection, in other words, it is to be *thoroughly made*. According to

90

HOPKINS' SANCTITY

Catholic theology perfection demands a *substantial transformation* which is called first sanctifying grace and then beatitude, it involves the mysterious co-working of grace and free-will. To go into this question further would be a digression. What I want to emphasize is that for Hopkins, life was a continuous substantial progress toward perfection. He believed this, he lived this, this is what he wrote.

I think it can be shown that the beliefs and practices of most modern poets more or less exclude perfection, and that insofar as perfection is shut out the poetry suffers. The writings as well as writers should be judged in terms of substantial action. For writings are dependent on writers although there never will be any laws for judging one by the other. A number of famous modern poems are specifically about human perfection: *An Essay on Man, An Ode to Evening, The Prelude, On a Grecian Urn, The Scholar Gypsy, Among School Children, The Wasteland.* Indeed, there is very little writing on anything else. I think if any of these poems are set against *The Wreck of the Deutschland* or Hopkins' last sonnets, they appear a little abstract and superficial. The reason is not that the writers did not experience what they wrote about, they all did; but their experience is confined to one faculty: reason, imagination or memory. They are rationalists or romantics.

Hopkins has his faults. (1) He knew nature but he did not know too much about people. He met them sacramentally and at their occupations, but, in his poems at least, he shows little knowledge of their individuality and character. When he writes about the sacramental experiences of occupational types (*Felix Randall*), or, better, about his own experiences of nature or God, he is on solid ground. Sometimes he slips. I have never altogether liked his nuns and sailors in *The Wreck of the Deutschland*. Perhaps this is why *Harry Plowman* and *Tom's Garland* are so heavy. (2) Hopkins' rhythms even when he is not writing sprung-rhythm have the effect of a hyperthyroid injection. As we know from the letters and personal anecdotes, he lived in a state of exhilaration. But in some poems we feel that the intensity is mannered, in others we could wish for more variety. I agree with most of Mr. Mc-Luhan's excellent analysis of *The Windhover*, but it is perhaps a limitation that the last six lines are forced by their rhythm, almost in spite of themselves, to rival the simple physical intensity of the octet. The versatility, however, of these rhythms within their limitations is miraculous. They are more a personal limitation than a fault. (3) There is something in style that is very close to conversation. The conversation may be either genteel or colloquial, but it must have a supple gravity and scope as well as color. Masterpieces of style are *The Wife of Bath's Prologue,* Villon's *Testament,* Shakespeare's great tragedies, the best ballads, Milton's sonnets, the lyrics of Donne, Herbert, Marvell, the later tracts and satires of Pope and Dryden, and some of Hardy; the great recent master is Yeats. Hopkins belongs to this tradition; infrequently his lines collapse in a styleless exuberance:

> This was that fell capsize
> As half she had righted and hoped to rise
> Death teeming in at her port-holes
> Raced down decks, round messes of mortals.

HOPKINS' SANCTITY

Messes of mortals! This is a murderous example of numb sprung-rhythm and alliteration. There are other lines that verge on this and are only saved by their strong, original feeling. In his last letter to Bridges, he writes: "The river is the Barrow, which the old Irish poets called the dumb Barrow. I call it burling Barrow Brown. Both descriptions are true." This sort of thing is common in the 19th and even 18th Centuries, and meter never entirely escapes it, but earlier it would have been uncommon. (4) Enough has been written about Hopkins' awkwardness, obscurity and syntactical violence. For such an innovator these were probably unavoidable. The best remedy, Hopkins' and Mr. Whitehall's, is a sensitive recital.

Hopkins' epitaph, I think, should run something like this. He wrote religious lyrics that are thoroughly of the 19th Century and yet are unsurpassed by anything written in the great ages of religion. He is probably the finest of English poets of nature, i.e., of inanimate creation. Along with Dante, Villon, Ben Jonson, Donne, Herbert and Milton, he is one of the very few personal or substantially active poets. Besides being an innovator, he worked at least four different traditions, the alliterative, the Miltonic, the metaphysical and the Keatsian-romantic. According to Mr. Whitehall, he will perhaps be known as the restorer of recited verse. Yet his sermons and letters are as excellent as his poetry; and all his writing is just what he is: the work of his unique personality and holiness.

7. VICTORIAN HOPKINS

By Arthur Mizener

THE EMPHASIS ON THE ODDNESS AND MODERNNESS OF HOP-
kins' poetry has diminished considerably of late. This shift
began, perhaps, with Mr. Abbott's Introductions to the
Letters; it is marked in most of the contributors to the
Kenyon Review's symposium, especially in Mr. Warren's
very penetrating essay. This is certainly an important gain
toward a just evaluation of Hopkins, for much of the odd-
ness of his poetry, as he so often suggested himself, is a sur-
face phenomenon, not unimportant, but not more funda-
mental than the individual tone which is recognizable in
any poet, in Tennyson and Wordsworth quite as much as
in Browning and Whitman, to whom Hopkins, though not
on this ground, more than once compared himself ("As
he is a very great scoundrel this is not a pleasant confes-
sion").

Apart from his Catholic ideas (I do not mean to belittle

their importance for I think it very great; but there is nothing eccentric in thinking like a Catholic) and the intellectual precision he acquired from years of scholastic thought, Hopkins' thinking as a poet is neither eccentric nor especially complex. Much of it, furthermore, is that of the typical 19th Century Englishman. Indeed, his concern for the empire and his unquestioning acceptance of the superiority of Englishmen, except as they were corrupted by that "fatal and baleful influence," Gladstone, would be, like Tennyson's, comic were it not so obviously a very serious subject to him:

Do you know and realize what happened at Majuba Hill? 500 British troops . . . ran without offering hand to hand resistance before, it is said, 80 men. Such a thing was never heard in history. The disgrace in itself is unspeakable. (*Further Letters*, p. 146.)

But "The Soldier" and "What Shall I Do for the Land That Bred Me" speak for themselves on this subject. His social thinking in general, in fact, is very like Carlyle's, for all his dislike of Carlyle's Protestantism.

Nor, when he came to discuss poetry, did Hopkins very often complain about the confusion of poetic thinking so frequent in the poetry of his time. He was not, certainly, deeply impressed by Tennyson's thinking, though he felt that *In Memoriam* was a "divine work" as perhaps, considering his own religious career, it was only too easy for him to feel. But his main concern was for Tennyson's technical accomplishments, his vulgarity ("Not only *Locksley Hall* but *Maud* is an ungentlemanly row"), and his lack of inscape ("He shd. have called [his Idylls] *Charades from the Middle Ages* (dedicated by permission to H. R.

95

H. etc.)"). He was plainly impressed by Patmore's substance, if not always by his technique, and in so far as any everyday human world appears in Hopkins' poems it is the domestic, Trollopean world of Patmore with what Gosse called, not quite fairly, its "girls that smell of bread and butter." The fragment of "Richard" is a case and "The Brothers" another. He was even inclined to think Patmore sometimes too liberal, as when he has a wife call her husband lord "by courtesy." Hopkins protested:

But he *is* her lord, . . . And now pernicious doctrines and practice are abroad and the other day the papers said a wretched being refused in church to say the words "and obey". . . (*Further Letters,* p. 162.)

With Browning whom he found very offensive ("The Brownings are very fine too in their ghastly way") it was, as with Tennyson, the tone rather than the Victorian habits of thought which disturbed Hopkins:

Now he has got . . . a way of talking (and making his people talk) with the air and spirit of a man bouncing up from table with his mouth full of bread and cheese and saying that he meant to stand no blasted nonsense. . . . The effect of this style is frigid bluster. (*Letters to Dixon,* p. 74.)

This is neither the thinking nor the tone of voice of a poet in rebellion against his time, an anachronism out of the 20th or the 17th Century. Nor, surely, do Hopkins' feelings suggest anything of the kind. Apart, again, from the emphasis on specifically Catholic sentiments, they are typical Victorian feelings. The love of nature is strongly marked. Hopkins' life was filled, more even than one gathers from Hallam's *Memoir* that Tennyson's was, with the minute and loving observation of nature. There is no reason to suppose that the journal gives us an exhaustive account of Hopkins' interests; in fact we know it does not. But making every allowance for this distortion of the evidence, it still remains almost incredible how much of his time was spent in remarking the details of sunsets, flowers and waves.

Like Keats he had a most intense sensuous awareness of it to support this admirably objective and painstaking observation of nature, and as in Keats's case a part of him always encouraged and cultivated this awareness. This is, I suppose, the most obvious thing about his poetry and hardly needs illustrating, though the extent to which it contributed to his feeling that poetry was "unprofessional" is not so clear. We do know, from the famous school-boy experiment in going without water, that he felt a need to demonstrate his ability to sacrifice everything to a single end, a need which his age both felt and admired generally. In his early verse he applied this feeling to poetry through an adoption of the Grecian Urn fancy: "Shape nothing, lips, be lovely-dumb." But in the end it was St. Ignatius' doctrine which held the mature man:

Whence it follows, that man ought to make use of them ["the other things on the face of the earth"] just so far as they help him to attain his end, and that he ought to withdraw himself from them just so far as they hinder him.

On the whole this doctrine seems to have satisfied Hopkins. This is not to say he did not suffer under it or that his sense of the tragic conflict within man did not sometimes reach a point perilously close to plain rebellion.

There is little to be gained, I think, by pretending that he was perfectly at ease in his religion all his life: he was not the kind of man who would have been perfectly at ease all his life in any position. But as he remarked with such quiet force to Dixon: "And beyond that I can say with St. Peter: To whom shall I go? *Tu verba vitae aeternae habes.*" (p. 75.)

2

Hopkins was, then, if this account be just, a Victorian with a special temperamental intensity of sensuous awareness and a special inclination toward that kind of asceticism which counterbalances it. Like Keats he hated the frivolity of dogmatic "goodness": "beautiful as those are [Wordsworth's sonnets] they have an odious goodness and neckcloth about them which half throttles their beauty." (*Letters to Bridges*, p. 38.) [1] Like Keats, too, he had an instinctive tragic sense of life; and as in the case of Keats this was sometimes intensified in him by illness. As a Victorian Hopkins was conscious in his own right of all the problems which confronted the Victorian personality with particular force: the obsessive sensuous appeal of nature; the logical consequence of this appeal, its tendency to generate a special romantic version of the argument from design which led so frequently either to some sort of pantheism or through liberalism to confusion; the enormous temptation to resort to the individual feeling as a source of truth, which was apparently both a natural im-

---

[1] "We hate poetry that has a palpable design upon us, and, if we do not agree, seems to put its hands into its breeches pockets." Keats to Reynolds, February 3, 1818.

pulse and a necessary recourse of the Victorian mind confronted by the evidences of science.

All this is not to say that Hopkins was not, in a sense, an eccentric. The very essence of reality was for him the unique individual quality of things, the inner pattern of being which he called "inscape," and he was as much concerned with this aspect of himself, this pattern of personality, as he was with this aspect of things outside himself. His poems are accounts of the instress, the felt experience, of inscapes and are, therefore, themselves inscapes of Hopkins. This is merely to say that he was an individualist, in the 19th Century sense of that word, of the most marked kind. No one knew this better than he did:

Now it is the virtue of design, pattern, or inscape to be distinctive and it is the vice of distinctiveness to become queer. This vice I cannot have escaped. (*Letters to Bridges,* p. 66.)

But eccentricity, individualism in this sense, was a 19th Century and especially a British habit. It was what generated among the poets the belief that "every true poet . . . must be original and originality a condition of poetic genius" (*Further Letters,* p. 222); and Henry Adams was so impressed by it that he persuaded himself the English character would always be impenetrable to an outsider.

This conviction that reality resides ultimately in the personal and felt awareness of things is common, in one form or another, to Keats ("O for a Life of Sensations rather than of Thoughts!"), to Tennyson ("And like a man in wrath the heart/ Stood up and answer'd, 'I have felt.'"), and to the Pateresque Hedonism of the Nineties ("those impressions of the individual mind to which, for each one of us, experience dwindles down"). This conviction Hopkins shared in his own way. "I find myself," he wrote in the Comments on the Spiritual Exercises of St. Ignatius Loyola,

both as man and as myself something most determined and distinctive, at pitch, more distinctive and higher pitched than anything else I see. . . . And when I ask where does all this throng and stack of being, so rich, so distinctive, so important, come from / nothing I see can answer me. . . . And this is much more true . . . when I consider my selfbeing, my consciousness and feeling of myself, that taste of myself, of *I* and *me* above and in all things, which is more distinctive than the taste of ale or alum, more distinctive than the smell of walnut leaf or camphor. . . . Nothing else in nature comes near this unspeakable stress of pitch, distinctiveness, and selving, this selfbeing of my own. (*Notebooks,* p. 309.)

It is the forgèd feature finds me; it is the rehearsal
Of own, of abrupt self there so thrusts on, so throngs the ear.
(*Poems,* 21.)

For this conviction Hopkins found, or believed he found, support in Duns Scotus: "Is not this pitch or whatever we call it then [he has just called it also "self, personality"] the same as Scotus's *ecceitas?*" (*Notebooks,* p. 328.) This goes far, as a number of writers have pointed out, to explain Hopkins' enthusiasm for Scotus, though Hopkins was much moved also by Scotus' alleged disputation in support of the Immaculate Conception.

It was only, then, in this representative way that Hopkins was eccentric, but this is not the kind of eccentricity we ordinarily think of today when we discuss this subject. Somewhere in the back of our minds we have a model derived from the 17th Century, so that as a consequence we think of eccentricity as being a matter rather of the poet's

100

fundamental conception of reality than of his way of realizing it. In this way Hopkins was not eccentric at all but a man of his time.

What did make Hopkins almost unique in his time was his Catholicism, not an emotional, antiquarian, or hedonistic Catholicism—these were fairly common in the period—but a precise, logical and deeply felt knowledge of Catholic doctrine to which, on the whole, he successfully disciplined both his thinking and his feeling. For him the sensuous beauty of the world was neither to be denied nor suppressed but accepted and subordinated to "God's better beauty, grace":

> What do then? how meet beauty? Merely meet it; own
> Home at heart, heaven's sweet gift; then leave, let that alone.
> Yea, wish that thought, wish all, God's better beauty, grace.
> (*Poems*, 38.)

So he spoke of human beauty, and he said the same thing of the beauty of nature almost every time he mentioned it. The clearness of his thought, however odd his words, on the immanence and transcendence of God saved him from any of the jerry-built cosmologies to which the Victorians and Romantics had frequently to resort in trying to deal with their intense awareness of nature:

Neither do I deny that God is so deeply present to everything . . . that it would be impossible for him but for his infinity not to be identified with them or, from the other side, impossible but for his infinity so to be present to them. (*Notebooks,* p. 316.)

. . . a sovereignty that heeds but hides, bodes but abides.

And his sometimes profoundly painful belief that the whole meaning of personality was not to realize itself but to realize Christ in itself saved him from the various absurd extremes of individualism which were tried by other late Victorians:

> Acts in God's eye what in God's eye he is—
> Christ—for Christ plays in ten thousand places,
> Lovely in limbs, and lovely in eyes not his
> To the Father through the features of men's faces.
> (*Poems*, 34.)

Perhaps, like St. Ignatius and his followers who were going to the Holy Land to live Christ's life as literally as they could, Hopkins never got there; but he never went anywhere else.

There is nothing, I should think, especially esoteric about this kind of thinking. Hopkins was a scholarly and thoughtful man but neither a philosopher nor a mystic. He belonged by temperament to that class of 19th Century poets who combined intense sensuousness and seriousness and he happened into an Oxford and among a group of friends to whom the Catholic Church had a great appeal. Because the scholastic discipline is both inclusive and subtle and because Hopkins lived and thought it most of his life, it gave his talents as a poet a design and a precision which it is difficult to imagine their acquiring from any other source. At best, by giving it a metaphysical point of reference, it gave greater intensity to his sensuous apprehension of the world:

Suppose God showed us in a vision the whole world enclosed first in a drop of water, allowing everything to be seen in its native colours; then the same in a drop of Christ's blood, by which everything whatever was turned to scarlet, keeping nevertheless mounted in the scarlet its own colour too. (From an unpublished ms. quoted by Pick, pp. 44–5.)

Above all, it provided a solid framework of ideas for all his poems.

3

The basic sensibility of Hopkins' poetry, then, is a Victorian sensibility, given a precision very nearly unique for its time by a lifetime's habituation to scholastic thought. This precision complemented, I think, but never fused with, that minute and objective observation of nature which he shared with such writers as Ruskin and Tennyson and which was the outlet for his loving and sensuous awareness of the physical world around him. What Mr. Eliot said, perhaps in derogation (though it need not be so said) of Tennyson and Browning and might well have said also of any number of other Victorian poets is equally true of Hopkins: "It is the difference between the intellectual and the reflective poet. Tennyson and Browning are poets, and they think; but they do not feel their thought as immediately as the odour of a rose." The basic structure of Hopkins' lyrics is a description followed by a comment, an application. They are, for all their intensity, poems of reflection, in the best sense of the word rhetorical rather than dramatic. Occasionally he indulged in the kind of naked symbolism by which the lion, for instance, becomes God's strength and conducts himself accordingly, without regard for the natural habits of lions. At best this practice made for the fantastic kind of poetry we associate with Crashaw:

103

> And makes, O marvellous!
> New Nazareths in us,
> Where we shall yet conceive
> Him morning, noon, and eve.
> (*Poems,* 37.)

But otherwise Hopkins' nature is not, as Mr. Tate says, mythologized. If, however, the kind of fusion of meaning and sensuous symbol which Mr. Eliot admires does not occur in Hopkins, it is nevertheless true that he knew exactly what the relation between nature and man was:

The sun and the stars shining glorify God. . . . They glorify God, *but they do not know it.* . . . But men can know God, *can mean to give him glory.* (*Notebooks,* pp. 302–3.)

> Earth, sweet Earth, sweet landscape, with leavès throng
> And louchèd low grass, heaven that dost appeal
> To, with no tongue to plead, no heart to feel. . . .
>   And what is Earth's eye, tongue, or heart else, where
> Else, but in dear and dogged man?
>
> (*Poems,* 35.)

In terms of this complementary relationship between the two, Hopkins understood both nature and man:

As we drove home the stars came out thick: I leant back to look at them and my heart opening more than usual praised our Lord to and in whom all that beauty comes home. (*Notebooks,* p. 205.)

It was because his observation of nature was so minute, his response to it so intense, his conception of man's relation to it and to God so precise, that Hopkins was able to bring this kind of poem to a point of perfection unequalled in his time. He almost never wrote the kind of poem in which description and observation are at best related only by a mood, and a mood not infrequently containing un-resolved ambiguities, as Tennyson did in poems like "Oenone," "The Lotus Eaters," and "Maud." He seldom wrote the kind of poem in which congruence of mood is supported by loose analogy as Arnold did in a poem in other ways so fine as "Dover Beach." Yet the essential pat-tern of his poems is quite clearly this pattern. Precisely as "Dover Beach" turns, structurally, on the lines

> The Sea of Faith
> Was once, too, at the full. . . .

so, for example, "Spelt from Sibyl's Leaves" turns on

> Heart, you round me right
> With: Óur évening is over us; óur night whélms, whélms ánd will
> end us.
> Only the beak-leaved boughs dragonish damask the tool-smooth
> bleak light; black,
> Ever so black on it. Óur tale, O óur oracle!

Hopkins also devised a way of writing the description of nature which constitutes the first element in this typical structure such that he was able to realize its purpose more fully than most of the poets of his time. This way of writ-ing consisted of a new rhythm, the echo of which he "had long had haunting [his] ear" even when he wrote "The Wreck of the Deutschland," and a new diction. The new diction was partly the outgrowth of the new rhythm and the alliteration, assonance and internal rhyming which, as Mr. Whitehall has shown, are necessary to its structure. It grew partly, also, from Hopkins' precise if random scholarly interest in the special speech characteristics of particular localities, an interest which was merely one

105

manifestation of his delight in all that gave evidence of the unique "taste" of things. The sources of both the rhythm and the vocabulary—"a sort of Platonic ideal of idiomatic language" as Miss Phare calls it—may be traced in the *Letters* and *Notebooks,* but not their causes.

Between them these two things have had more to do, I suppose, than anything else with Hopkins' reputation for eccentricity, and they are certainly highly individual. But the individualism which led him to them is Victorian: the same impulse was at work in Browning and Carlyle (Hopkins and Carlyle even shared a now puzzling interest in fantastic etymologies). In Hopkins' case, as perhaps never in Carlyle's and not always in Browning's, this impulse was not exercised for its own sake but disciplined to a real poetic need. Because Hopkins was intent on communicating the inscape, the felt pattern or design which was at the heart of a thing's reality for him, he desperately needed a way of speaking which would allow him to linger over, to stress for the listener, the quality of things. Therefore the typical unit of statement with him is a patterned and dynamically balanced series of sensuous notations:

Towery city and branchy between towers;
Cuckoo-echoing, bell-swarmèd, lark-charmèd, rock-racked, river-
    rounded;
The dapple-eared lily below thee; that country and town did
Once encounter in, here coped and poisèd powers.

(*Poems,* 20.)

This is clearly a device for holding thought in suspense in order that feeling may be stressed, and it appears in perhaps its purest and, to the inexperienced reader, most dis-

106

tressing form in poems like "The Leaden Echo and the Golden Echo":

How to kéep—is there ány any, is there none such, nowhere known
        some, bow or brooch or braid or brace, láce, latch or catch
        or key to keep
Back beauty, keep it. . . .

"*Back*," he wrote Bridges, "is not pretty, but it gives that feeling of physical restraint which I want." (*Letters to Bridges*, p. 162.) And this is exactly the purpose of the accumulation of clasps, ties and locks in the previous line; they give emphasis to the feeling by repeating it in an overwhelming number of contexts so that it "whelms, whelms and will end us" if we read it right and share his profound feeling for the structure of things:

The ashtree growing in the corner of the garden was felled. It was lopped first: I heard the sound and looking out and seeing it maimed there came at that moment a great pang and I wished to die and not to see the inscapes of the world destroyed any more. (*Notebooks*, p. 174; compare "Binsey Poplars.")

A better instance of the interlocking of rhythm and diction to a single purpose would be difficult to find. Even in poems primarily of statement Hopkins used this device of accumulation to mark the exact emphasis which the experience he is recording had for him:

Have fair fallen, O fair, fair have fallen, so dear
To me, so arch-especial a spirit as heaves in Henry Purcell. . . .
                                                    (*Poems*, 21.)

Often all that keeps this potentially grotesque lingering over a single feeling from becoming either a dead list as do so many of Whitman's or an intolerable excrescence on the poem's thought is the wonderful rhetorical control of the rhythm. It seems to me an open question whether the necessities of Hopkins' sensibility, with its need for repetition, led to his adoption of Sprung Rhythm or the necessities of Sprung Rhythm, as Mr. Whitehall suggests, led to the repetitions. In either case, however, there was another reason for the new rhythm. For Hopkins the poem in itself was an inscape, a thing which must be experienced. The rhythm therefore had to have a shape, a design which would bring it home to the reader with the maximum instress, and the best model for such a design, he knew, was actual speech:

Why do I employ sprung rhythm at all? Because it is the nearest to the rhythm of prose, that is the native and natural rhythm of speech, the least forced, the most rhetorical and emphatic of all possible rhythms. . . . (*Letters to Bridges,* p. 46.)

However much Hopkins crowded a sentence with repetitions, it never lost the cadence of actual speech; the sound of the voice speaking it is always there in the reader's ear to give the poems their incomparable immediacy. It was because of the absolute need he felt to sustain this effect that Hopkins resorted to those turns of phrase from idiomatic speech which so shocked Bridges and which often seem to modern readers to make for unnecessary obscurities. To Bridges with his love of "a continuous literary decorum" Hopkins could only say: "but take breath and read it with the ears, as I always wish to be read, and my verse becomes all right." (*Letters to Bridges,* p. 79.)

It becomes, indeed, something a good deal more than

108

all right, something often magnificent and always vivid and alive. And this was a result Hopkins could achieve only by the use of an idiomatic syntax which is actually more unexpected than obscure. The quatrain quoted from the Duns Scotus sonnet above (p. 106) offers a simple example. In the opening half of the third line Hopkins uses an abbreviated direct statement as a vocative: its meaning is in exact parallel with the meaning of the first two lines. This is grammatically loose, but a very common practice in speech and one which gives the ear no trouble, however much it may bother the eye. This is followed by an even more colloquial turn of phrase, for the *that* with which it begins is a relative governed by *in:* "the place in which country and town did once meet." (The same construction occurs in the quotation from poem 35 on page 104.) The final phrase of the passage also involves a colloquial ellipsis: "and where as equal powers they coped with each other and stood poised in dynamic balance." This mastery of the syntax of the spoken rather than the written language served Hopkins as a means for making his poems not only rhetorical wholes but compressed, economical and, as he called it, "explosive" wholes, despite the disruptive pressure of the repetitions.

4

The terms of Hopkins' achievement as a poet were the complementary structure which was determined by his understanding of feeling and thought and the cumulative style which his preoccupation with the unique quality of things dictated. In these terms Hopkins reached an unsurpassed exactness and subtlety both of meaning in general and of image in particular. He was acutely aware of this aspect of his contemporaries' work, describing one rather harmless image of Browning's as "monstrous" and displaying an inexhaustible interest in the minutiae of the poems Bridges, Dixon and Patmore sent him. He had little patience with complaints against the kind of difficulty which arises from colloquial compression ("The sonnet (I say it snorting) aims at being intelligible." *Letters to Bridges*, p. 293), but he was always anxious to confront charges of ambiguity honestly (see for example the remarks on the Purcell sonnet, *Letters to Bridges*, p. 83).

The kind of concentration and intensity which resulted from the combination of this exactitude of image with the precision of his thought and structure was Hopkins' great achievement. It is worth examining carefully, for it is a rare achievement at any time and an especially rare one in the late 19th Century. A stanza from "The Wreck of the Deutschland" will illustrate it.

> I am soft sift
> In an hourglass—at the wall
> Fast, but mined with a motion, a drift,
> And it crowds and it combs to the fall;
> I steady as a water in a well, to a poise, to a pane,
> But roped with always, all the way down from the tall
> Fells or flanks of the voel, a vein
> Of the gospel proffer, a pressure, a principle, Christ's gift.

There are oddities here which can, I think, be ascribed only to Hopkins' isolation as a poet. He did not dare to change anything on the judgment of one reader, especially

110

one who, for all his good will, was as little sympathetic as Bridges; and Bridges was practically his only reader. "I cannot think of altering anything. Why shd. I? I do not write for the public. You are my public and I hope to convert you." (*Letters to Bridges*, p. 46.) But no man's judgment is infallible in such delicate matters and for want of the help he did not have Hopkins retained such usages as "pane," "roped," and "voel" which are oddities rather than difficulties demanded by thought and feeling, "queer" in Hopkins' own words (see p. 99) rather than "distinctive."

Otherwise this stanza is a magnificent example of Hopkins' kind of complex precision. If I read it correctly, he is contrasting his natural self with what he is because of Christ's gift. The image of the hourglass fits the first of these two ideas very closely, and is carefully worked out both as a description of the object of comparison and for the feeling Hopkins wishes to evoke. No one knew better than Hopkins the imperfections of man and his unsteadiness of will; "And the drunkards go on drinking, the filthy, as the scripture says, are filthy still: human nature is so inveterate." (*Letters to Bridges*, p. 110.) It was his own claim that Catholicism alone allowed one to look on these things steadily without despair. In any event, the knowledge of how man shifts and changes in the traitorous, almost imperceptible, and yet in the end apparently accelerating movement of time is here in the ominous overtones of "soft sift" and "mined," in the implications of unsteady will in "drift," in the terrifying rush of "And it crowds and it combs to the fall." As Hopkins wrote, half humorously, to his sister:

111

As for me I will say no more than this, that I have prescribed my self twenty-four hourglasses a day (which I take even during sleep, such is the force of habit) and that even this does not stop the ravages of time. (*Further Letters,* p. 41.)

Perhaps the subdued terror in this first image comes most from the impression it gives of run-away motion, of movement not balanced or poised. In any event, an acute sense of movement was for Hopkins the heart of reality, and the dramatic balance of movements the thing he responded to most; it was, for him, fulfillment. He spoke, for example, of the mystery of the Trinity for Catholics as

leaving them all their lives balancing whether they have three heavenly friends or one—not that they have any doubt on the subject, but that their knowledge leaves their minds swinging; poised, but on the quiver. And this might be the ecstasy of interest, one would think. (*Letters to Bridges,* p. 187–8.)

This "ecstasy of interest" is everywhere in the poems and had an inexhaustible fascination for Hopkins. It is perhaps at its most magnificent in the octet of "The Windhover." Here it constitutes the main appeal of the windhover in his riding "Of the rolling level underneath him steady air" on which he is so exquisitely poised; it dominates the imagery of the horse "in his ecstasy" taut against the rein, of the skate sweeping, tense against the hard ice, in a smooth curve; and it is realized in every rise and fall of the "roped" and "laced" curve of rhythm which comes finally to rest on that completely idiomatic yet perfectly stressed exclamation: "The achieve of, the mastery of the thing!"

This same feeling for the profound rightness of balanced forces is embodied in the image of the well which fills the latter half of the stanza from "The Wreck of the Deutsch-

112

land." The image almost certainly had, however, the further support of a particular experience of St. Winefred's Well, a knowledge of which helps to fill out the perhaps overcompressed figure of "a vein/ Of the gospel proffer":

The sight of the water in the well as clear as glass, greenish like beryl or aquamarine, trembling at the surface with the force of the springs . . . held my eyes to it . . . the sensible thing so naturally and gracefully uttering the spiritual reason of its being (which is all in true keeping with the story of St. Winefred's death and recovery) and the spring in place leading back the thoughts by its spring in time to its spring in eternity: even now the stress and buoyancy and abundance of the water is before my eyes. (*Notebooks*, p. 214.)

Thus Hopkins gives us in the second half of the stanza an image, *not* of a surface mined from beneath and sinking away, at first gradually, almost imperceptibly, and then with the terrible rush of a breaking wave. He gives us rather an image of a surface held steady, poised, by the pressure of the springs which fall all the way from the top of the mountain to flow into the well from beneath and, without breaking the tension of its surface, set it trembling, "rope" and interlace it, with movement. It is a similar pressure, "Christ's gift," which alone holds man's self "to a poise, to a pane."

It seems to me that the consequences of studying Hopkins' poems anew in the light of the *Letters* and *Notebooks* is inescapable. It is a conviction that Hopkins is Victorian, in a good many respects obviously Victorian; and that it is only the integrity and skill with which he fulfilled the other impulses of his nature which tends to hinder our recognition of the fact that even in these impulses he represents his time. This conviction is, I think, explicitly or implicitly endorsed by all the contributors to the *Kenyon Review's* symposium. If we cannot say, as perhaps we cannot, that Hopkins is the greatest of the Victorian poets, it is only because of the smallness of his output. He is certainly the most satisfying of them.

8. METAPHYSICAL ISOLATION

By F. R. Leavis

THAT HOPKINS HAS A PERMANENT PLACE AMONG THE ENGLISH poets may now be taken as established beyond challenge: academic scholarship has canonized him, and the love of "a continuous literary decorum" has forgotten the terms in which it was apt to express itself only a decade ago. It is now timely to ask just what that place is. Perhaps, indeed, formal evaluation may be judged a needless formality, the nature and significance of Hopkins's work, once it has been fairly looked at, not being very notably obscure. However, the centenary year of his birth seems a proper occasion for attempting a brief explicit summing-up.

A poet born in 1844 was a Victorian: if one finds oneself proffering this chronological truism today, when the current acceptance of Hopkins goes with a recognition that something has happened in English poetry since Bridges' taste was formed, it is less likely to be a note of irony, invoking a background contrast for Hopkins, than an insistence, or the preface to it, on the essential respects in which Hopkins was, even in his originality, *of* his time. His school poem, *A Vision of Mermaids*, shows him starting very happily in a Keatsian line, a normal young contemporary of Tennyson, Matthew Arnold and Rossetti—in the association of which three names, it will perhaps be granted, the idea of "Victorian poet" takes on sufficient force and definition to give that "normal" its point. The element of Keats in Hopkins is radical and very striking:

> Palate, the hutch of tasty lust,
> Desire not to be rinsed with wine:
> The can must be so sweet, the crust
> So fresh that come in fasts divine!
>
> Nostrils, your careless breath that spend
> Upon the stir and keep of pride,
> What relish shall the censers send
> Along the sanctuary side!
>
> O feel-of-primrose hands, O feet
> That want the yield of plushy sward,
> But you shall walk the golden street
> And you unhouse and house the Lord.

These stanzas come from an "Early Poem" printed by Bridges immediately before *The Wreck of the Deutschland*. A contemporary reader, if we can imagine it published at the time of writing, might very well have judged that this very decided young talent was to be distinguished from among his fellow Victorian poets by his unique possession, in an age pervaded by Keatsian aspirations and in-

116

fluences, of the essential Keatsian strength. Such a Victorian reader might very well have pronounced him, this strength clearly being native and inward, unmistakably a poet born—a poet incomparably more like Keats, the poet's poet (Keats was something like that for the Tennysonian age), than the derivatively Keatsian could make themselves. Actually, the body of the mature work—*The Wreck of the Deutschland* onward—in which Hopkins's distinctive bent and his idiosyncrasy develop to the full doesn't prompt us with Keats's name so obviously. Yet the same strength, in its developed manifestations, is there.

It is a strength that gives Hopkins notable advantages over Tennyson and Matthew Arnold as a "nature poet." This description is Mr. Eliot's (see *After Strange Gods,* p. 48), and it is applicable enough for one to accept it as a way of bringing out how much Hopkins belongs to the Victorian tradition. Nature, beauty, transience—with these he is characteristically preoccupied:

> Margaret, are you grieving
> Over Goldengrove unleaving?
> Leaves, like the things of man, you
> With you fresh thoughts care for, can you?
> Ah! as the heart grows older
> It will come to such sights colder
> By and by, nor spare a sigh
> Though worlds of wanwood leafmeal lie;
> And yet you will weep and know why.
> Now no matter, child, the name:
> Sorrow's springs are the same.
> Nor mouth had, no, nor mind, expressed
> What heart heard of, ghost guessed:
> It is the blight man was born for,
> It is Margaret you mourn for.

117

Here the distinctiveness and the idiosyncrasy might seem hardly to qualify the Victorian normality of the whole (though Bridges couldn't permit the second couplet—see the improved poem that, modestly claiming no credit, he prints in *The Spirit of Man*). In

> What heart heard of, ghost guessed,

where the heart, wholly taken up in the hearing, becomes it, as the "ghost" becomes the guessing, we have, of course, an example of a kind of poetic action or enactment that Hopkins developed into a staple habit of his art. As we have it, this use of assonantal progression, here, its relation to the sensibility and technique of

> Palate, the hutch of tasty lust

is plain. So too is the affinity between this last-quoted line and the "bend with apples the moss'd cottage trees" in which the robust vitality of Keats's sensuousness shows itself in so un-Tennysonian, and so essentially poetic, a strength of expressive texture.

Hopkins was born—and died—in the age of Tennyson. This fact has an obvious bearing on the deliberateness with which Hopkins, starting with that peculiar genius, set himself to develop and exploit the modes and qualities of expression illustrated—the distinctive expressive resources of the English language ("English must be kept up"). The age in poetry *was* Tennyson's; and an age for which the ambition "to bring English as near the Italian as possible" seems a natural and essentially poetic one, is an age in which the genius conscious enough to form a contrary ambition is likely to be very conscious and very contrary. That he was consciously bent on bringing back into poetry the life and strength of the living, the spoken, language is explicit—the confirmation was pleasant to have, though hardly necessary—in the *Letters* (to Bridges, LXII): "it seems to me that the poetical language of the age shd. be the current language heightened, to any degree heightened and unlike it, but not (I mean normally: passing freaks and graces are another thing) an obsolete one." His praise of Dryden (CLV), held by Bridges to be no poet, is well-known: "His style and rhythms lay the strongest stress of all our literature on the naked thew and sinew of the English language." This preoccupation, pursued by a Victorian poet intensely given to technical experiment, would go far to explain the triumphs of invention, the extravagances and the oddities of Hopkins's verse.

But this is not the whole story. His bent for technical experiment can be seen to have been inseparable from a special kind of interest in pattern—his own term was "inscape." Here we have a head of consideration that calls for some inquiry, though it can be left for the moment with this parenthetic recognition, to be taken up again in due course.

Meanwhile, demanding immediate notice, there is a head the postponement of which till now may have surprised the reader. It is impossible to discuss for long the distinctive qualities of Hopkins's poetry without coming to his religion. In the matter of religion, of course, he differs notably from both Tennyson and Matthew Arnold, and the relevance of the differences to the business of the literary critic is best broached by noting that they lead up

119

to the complete and startling antithesis confronting us when we place Hopkins by Rossetti. Here is Rossetti:

> Under the arch of Life, where love and death,
>   Terror and mystery, guard her shrine, I saw
>   Beauty enthroned; and though her gaze struck awe,
> I drew it in as simply as my breath.
> Hers are the eyes which, over and beneath,
>   The sky and sea bend on thee—which can draw,
>   By sea or sky or woman, to one law,
> The allotted bondman of her palm and wreath.
>
> This is that Lady Beauty, in whose praise
>   Thy voice and hand shake still—long known to thee
>   By flying hair and fluttering hem—the beat
>   Following her daily of thy heart and feet,
> How passionately and irretrievably,
> In what fond flight, how many ways and days!

This very representative poem illustrates very obviously the immediate relevance for the literary critic of saying that religion in Hopkins's poetry is something completely other than the religion of Beauty. Rossetti's shamelessly cheap evocation of a romantic and bogus Platonism—an evocation in which "significance" is vagueness, and profundity an uninhibited proffer of large drafts on a merely nominal account ("Life," "love," "death," "terror," "mystery," "Beauty"—it is a bankrupt's lavishness)—exemplifies in a gross form the consequences of that separation of feeling ("soul"—the source of "genuine poetry") from thinking which the Victorian tradition, in its "poetical" use of language, carries with it. The attendant debility is apparent enough in Tennyson and Arnold, poets who

120

often think they are thinking and who offer thought about
life, religion and morals: of Arnold in particular the point
can be made that what he offers poetically as thought is
dismissed as negligible by the standards of his prose.
When we come to the hierophant of Beauty, the dedicated
poet of the cult, predecessor of the Pater who formulated
the credo, we have something worse than debility. And
there is not only a complete nullity in respect of thought—
nullity made aggressively vulgar by a wordy pretentious-
ness (Rossetti is officially credited with "fundamental
brainwork"); the emotional and sensuous quality may be
indicated by saying that in Rossetti's verse we find nothing
more of the "hard gem-like flame" than in Pater's prose.

Hopkins is the devotional poet of a dogmatic Christi-
anity. For the literary critic there are consequent difficul-
ties and delicacies. But there is something that can be
seen, and said, at once: Hopkins's religious interests are
bound up with the presence in his poetry of a vigour of
mind that puts him in another poetic world from the other
Victorians. It is a vitality of thought, a vigour of the think-
ing intelligence, that is at the same time a vitality of con-
creteness. The relation between this kind of poetic life
and his religion manifests itself plainly in his addiction to
Duns Scotus, whom, rather than St. Thomas, traditionally
indicated for a Jesuit, he significantly embraced as his own
philosopher. Of the philosophy of Duns Scotus it must
suffice to say here that it lays a peculiar stress on the par-
ticular and actual, in its full concreteness and individu-
ality, as the focus of the real, and that its presence is felt
whenever Hopkins uses the word "self" (or some deriva-
tive verb) in his characteristic way. *Binsey Poplars* pro-

vides an instance where the significance for the literary
critic is obvious. The poplars are

> All felled, felled, are all felled,

and Hopkins's lament runs:

> O if we but knew what we do
>> When we delve or hew—
> Hack and rack the growing green!
>> Since country is so tender
> To touch, her being so slender,
> That, like this sleek and seeing ball
> But a prick will make no eye at all,
> Where we, even where we mean
>> To mend her we end her,
>> When we hew or delve:
> After-comers cannot guess the beauty been.
>> Ten or twelve, only ten or twelve
> Strokes of havoc unselve
>> The sweet especial scene,
> Rural scene, a rural scene
> Sweet especial rural scene.

All the beauties Hopkins renders in his poetry are
"sweet especial scenes," "selves" in the poignant signifi-
cance their particularity has for him. Time "unselves"
them;

> Nor can you long be, what you now are, called fair,
> Do what you may do, what, do what you may,
> And wisdom is early to despair.

The Victorian-romantic addicts of beauty and transience
cherish the pang as a kind of religiose-poetic sanction for
defeatism in the face of an alien actual world—a defeat-
ism offering itself as a spiritual superiority. Hopkins em-

braces transience as a necessary condition of any grasp of the real. The concern for such a grasp is there in the concrete qualities that give his poetry its vitality—which, we have seen, involves an energy of intelligence.

These qualities the literary critic notes and appraises, whether or not he knows any more about Duns Scotus than he can gather from the poetry. There is plainly a context of theological religion, and the devotional interest has plainly the kind of relation to the poetic qualities that has just been discussed. But the activities that go on within this context, even if they make Hopkins unlike Tennyson, Browning, Matthew Arnold, Rossetti and Swinburne, don't do so by making him in any radical way like T. S. Eliot. It is a framework of the given, conditioning the system of tensions established within it, and these are those of a devotional poet. We can hardly imagine Hopkins entertaining, even in a remotely theoretical way, the kind of preoccupation conveyed by Eliot when he says: ". . . I cannot see that poetry can ever be separated from something which I should call belief, and to which I cannot see any reason for refusing the name of belief, unless we are to shuffle names altogether. It should hardly be needful to say that it will not inevitably be orthodox Christian belief, although that possibly can be entertained, since Christianity will probably continue to modify itself, as in the past, into something that can be believed in (I do not mean *conscious* modifications like modernism etc., which always have the opposite effect). The majority of people live below the level of belief or doubt. It takes application and a kind of genius to believe anything, and to believe *anything* (I do *not* mean merely to believe in some 'reli-

123

gion') will probably become more and more difficult as time goes on." [*The Enemy,* January, 1927.] The stress of the "terrible sonnets" hasn't this kind of context. And Hopkins's habit is utterly remote from Eliot's extreme discipline of continence in respect of affirmation—the discipline involving that constructive avoidance of the conceptual currency which has its exposition in *Burnt Norton.* For Hopkins the truths are *there,* simply and irresistibly demanding allegiance; though it is no simple matter to make his allegiance real and complete (this seems at any rate a fair way of suggesting the difference).

His preoccupation with this frame is of a kind that leaves him in a certain obvious sense simple-minded:

> Here he knelt then in regimental red.
> Forth Christ from cupboard fetched, how fain I of feet
>   To his youngster take his treat!
> Low-latched in leaf-light housel his too huge godhead.

It is the simplicity of the single-minded and pure in heart. Its manifestations can be very disconcerting, and we are not surprised to learn that as a preacher he was apt, in his innocent unconsciousness, to put intolerable strains on the gravity of his congregation. It appears in the rime of the stanza immediately preceding that just quoted (it will be necessary, because of the run-over of the sense, to quote the two preceding):

> A bugler boy from barrack (it is over the hill
> There)—boy bugler, born, he tells me, of Irish
>   Mother to an English sire (he
> Shares their best gifts surely, fall how things will),

METAPHYSICAL ISOLATION

> This very very day came down to us after a boon he on
> My late being there begged of me, overflowing
>   Boon in my bestowing,
> Came, I say, this day to it—to a First Communion.

It takes a Bridges to find all, or most, of Hopkins's riming audacities unjustifiable; they are often triumphant successes in that, once the poem has been taken, they become inevitable, and, unlike Browning's ingenuities, cease to call attention to themselves (that in the first of these two stanzas is a passable ear-rime). Nevertheless there are a fair number of the order of *boon he on Communion,* and it has to be conceded more generally that the naivety illustrated has some part in the elaborations of his technique.

To say this, of course, is not to endorse Lord David Cecil's view that Hopkins is difficult because of his difficult way of saying simple things. It is relevant, but hardly necessary, to remark that for Hopkins his use of words is not a matter of *saying* things with them; he is preoccupied with what seems to him the poetic use of them, and that is a matter of making them do and be. Even a poet describable as "simple-minded" may justify some complexities of "doing" and "being." And if we predicate simplicity of Hopkins, it must be with the recognition that he has at the same time a very subtle mind.

The subtlety is apparent in the tropes, conceits and metaphorical symbolism that give his poetry qualities suggesting the seventeenth century rather than the nineteenth. He can be metaphysical in the full sense; as, for instance, he is, triumphantly, in the first part of *The Wreck of the Deutschland,* notably in stanzas 4 to 8. The radically metaphorical habit of mind and sensibility that, along with concrete strength from which it is inseparable, makes his "nature poetry" so different from Tennyson's and Matthew Arnold's, relates him to Herbert rather than to Eliot —it goes with the "frame" spoken of above. It is a habit of seeing things as charged with significance; "significance" here being, not a romantic vagueness, but a matter of explicit and ordered conceptions regarding the relations between God, man and nature. It is an inveterate habit of his mind and being, finding its intellectual formulation in Duns Scotus.

Of course, to be seventeenth-century in the time of Tennyson is a different matter from being it in the time of Herbert, Hopkins's unlikeness to whom involves a great deal more than the obvious difference of temperament. He is still more unlike Crashaw: his "metaphysical" audacity is the expression of a refined and disciplined spirit, and there is no temperamental reason why it shouldn't have been accompanied by something corresponding to Herbert's fine and poised *social* bearing. But behind Hopkins there is no Ben Jonson, and he has for contemporaries no constellation of courtly poets uniting the "metaphysical" with the urbane. His distinctiveness develops itself even in his prose, which has a dignified oddity such as one might have taken for affectation if it hadn't been so obviously innocent and unconscious.

Of the development of "distinctiveness" in verse he himself says, in a passage that gives us the word:

But as air, melody, is what strikes me most of all in music and design in painting, so design, pattern, or what I am in the habit of calling *inscape* is what I above all aim at in poetry. Now it is the virtue of design, pattern, or inscape to be distinctive, and it is the vice of distinctiveness to become queer. This vice I cannot have escaped. (*Poems*, 2nd Edition, p. 96.)

Isolation, he might have added, would favour the vice. But the peculiar development of the interest in pattern or "inscape" has, it may be suggested, a significance not yet touched on. We can't help relating it to a certain restriction in the nourishing interests behind Hopkins's poetry. It is as if his intensity, for lack of adequately answering substance, expressed itself in a kind of hypertrophy of technique, and in an excessive imputation of significance to formal pattern.

It may be replied that his concern for pattern in verse is paralleled by a concern for pattern (or "inscape" we had better say, since the word associates the idea of "pattern" with Hopkins's distinctive stress on the individuality or "self" of the object contemplated) in the sights—a tree, a waterfall, a disposition of clouds—that he renders from nature, renders in drawings as well as in verse and prose. But his interest in nature—to call attention to that is to make the same point again. In assenting, half-protestingly, to Mr. Eliot's description of him as a "nature poet" one is virtually recognizing that a significant limitation reveals itself when a poet of so remarkable a spiritual intensity, so intense a preoccupation with essential human problems, gives "nature"—the "nature" of the "nature poets"—so large a place in his poetry. What is revealed as limited, it will be said, is Hopkins's power to transcend the poetic climate of his age: in spite of the force of his originality he is a Victorian poet. This seems an unanswerable point.

127

But even here, in respect of his limitation, his distinctiveness comes out: the limitation goes with the peculiar limitation of experience attendant upon his early world-renouncing self-dedication.

> Elected Silence, sing to me
> And beat upon my whorlèd ear,
> Pipe me to pastures still and be
> The music that I care to hear.

> Shape nothing, lips; be lovely-dumb:
> It is the shut, the curfew sent
> From there where all surrenders come
> Which only makes you eloquent.

> Be shellèd, eyes, with double dark
> And find the uncreated light:
> This ruck and reel which you remark
> Coils, keeps, and teases simple sight.

>   ○   ○   ○

> And, Poverty, be thou the bride
> And now the marriage feast begun,
> And lily-coloured clothes provide
> Your spouse not laboured-at nor spun.

(This is the remainder of the "Early Poem," *The Habit of Perfection*, from which, in the opening of this essay, stanzas were quoted in illustration of Keatsian qualities.)

The force of this last point is manifest in the ardent naivety with which he idealizes his buglers, sailors, schoolboys and his England:

> England, whose honour O all my heart woos, wife
> To my creating thought . . .

128

METAPHYSICAL ISOLATION

Meeting him in 1882, his old schoolmaster, Dixon, says: "In so far as I can remember you are very like the boy of Highgate." But this unworldliness is of a different order from the normal other-worldliness of Victorian poetry. Addressing Hopkins, Matthew Arnold might, without the radical confusion symbolized in his Scholar Gypsy, have said:

> For early didst thou leave the world, with powers
> Fresh, undiverted to the world without.
>> Firm to their mark, not spent on other things;
> Free from the sick fatigue, the languid doubt . . .

The "firmness to the mark" is really there in Hopkins's poetry; the "mark" is not a mere postulated something that confers (we are to grant) a spiritual superiority upon the eternal week-ender who, "fluctuating idly without term or scope" among the attractions of the countryside, parallels in his indolent poetical way the strenuous aimlessness of the world where things are done. To Hopkins it might have been said with some point:

> Thou hadst *one* aim, *one* business, *one* desire.

Yet this unworldliness, different though it is from Victorian poetical other-worldliness, does unmistakably carry with it the limitation of experience. And in his bent for "nature" there is after all in Hopkins something of the poetical Victorian. It is a bent away from urban civilization, in the midst of which he spends his life, and which, naturally, he regards with repulsion:

> Generations have trod, have trod, have trod;
> And all is seared with trade; bleared, smeared with toil,
> And wears man's smudge and shares man's smell: the soil

Is bare now, nor can foot feel, being shod.
And for all this, nature is never spent;
　　There lives the dearest freshness deep down things; . . .

And in *The Sea and the Skylark* he says:

How these two shame this shallow and frail town!
　How ring right out our sordid turbid time,
Being pure! We, life's pride and cared-for crown,
Have lost that cheer and charm of earth's past prime;
Our make and making break, are breaking, down
　To man's last dust, drain fast towards man's first slime.

Towards these aspects of human life his attitude—he is very much preoccupied with them—is plain. But they have little more actual presence in his poetry than "this strange disease of modern life" has in Arnold's.

To come back now to his isolation—we have not yet taken full account of it. It is not merely a matter of his having had no support or countenance in accepted tradition, contemporary practice, and the climate of taste and ideas: he was isolated in a way peculiarly calculated to promote starvation of impulse, the over-developed and ingrown idiosyncrasy, and the sterile deadlock, lapsing into stagnation. As a convert he had with him a tide of the élite (he could feel); as a Catholic and a Jesuit he had his communities, the immediate and the wider. But from this all-important religious context he got no social endorsement as a poet: the episode of *The Wreck of the Deutschland*—"they dared not print it"—is all there is to tell, and it says everything; it came at the beginning and it was final. Robert Bridges, his life-long friend and correspondent, confidently and consistently discouraged him with

130

"water of the lower Isis": "your criticism is . . . only a protest memorializing me against my whole policy and proceedings" (xxxvii). As against this we can point, for the last seven years of Hopkins's life, to the enthusiasm of Canon Dixon, a good and generous man, but hardly transmutable by Hopkins's kind of need (or Hopkins's kind of humility) into an impressive critical endorsement or an adequate substitute for a non-existent public.

To these conditions the reaction of so tense and disciplined an ascetic is the reverse of Blake's: he doesn't become careless, but—"Then again I have of myself made verse so laborious" (LIII, to Bridges). (And here the following—from CLXVI—has an obvious relevance: "To return to composition for a moment: what I want there, to be more intelligible, smoother, and less singular, is an audience.") With the laboriousness goes the anguish of sterility registered in this sonnet—one of his finest poems:

> Thou art indeed just, Lord, if I contend
> With thee; but, sir, so what I plead is just.
> Why do sinners' ways prosper? and why must
> Disappointment all I endeavour end?
>   Wert thou my enemy, O thou my friend,
> How wouldst thou worse, I wonder, than thou dost
> Defeat, thwart me? Oh, the sots and thralls of lust
> Do in spare hours more thrive than I that spend,
> Sir, life upon thy cause. See, banks and brakes
> Now, leavèd how thick! lacèd they are again
> With fretty chervil, look, and fresh wind shakes
> Them; birds build—but not I build; no, but strain,
> Time's eunuch, and not breed one work that wakes.
> Mine, O thou lord of life, send my roots rain.

That there is a relation between this state of mind and

his isolation, the absence of response, he himself knows: "There is a point with me in matters of any size," he writes (CXXIX, to Bridges) "when I must absolutely have encouragement as much as crops rain; afterwards I am independent." The recurrence of the metaphor is significant, and the passage is clearly to be related to this other passage, itself so clearly related to the sonnet: "if I could but get on, if I could but produce work, I should not mind its being buried, silenced, and going no farther; but it kills me to be time's eunuch and never to beget" (CXXX). And again, he writes (CLVII): "All impulse fails me: I can give myself no reason for not going on. Nothing comes: I am a eunuch—but it is for the kingdom of heaven's sake." About the failure of impulse we are certainly in a position to say something.

It seems reasonable to suppose that if he had had the encouragement he lacked he would have devoted to poetry a good deal of the energy that (for the last years of his life a painfully conscientious Professor of Greek) he distributed, in a strenuous dissipation that undoubtedly had something to do with his sense of being time's eunuch and never producing, between the study of music, musical composition, drawing, and such task-work as writing a "popular account of Light and Ether." [1] For he was certainly a born writer. This is apparent in the *Letters* in ways we could hardly have divined from the poetry. Consider, for instance, the distinguished naturalness, the sensitive vivacity, the flexibility, and the easy sureness of touch of such representative passages as the following:

[1] "Popular is not quite the word: it is not meant to be easy reading" (XXXV, to Dixon).

METAPHYSICAL ISOLATION

Tomorrow morning I shall have been three years in Ireland, three hard wearing wasted years. (I met the blooming Miss Tynan again this afternoon. She told me that when she first saw me she took me for 20 and some friends of hers for 15; but it won't do: they should see my heart and vitals, all shaggy with the whitest hair). In those I have done God's will (in the main) and many examination papers.

There was a lovely and passionate scene (for about the space of the last trump) between me and a tallish gentleman (I daresay he was a cardsharper) in your carriage who was by way of being you; I smiled, I murmured with my lips at him, I waved farewells, but he would not give in, till with burning shame (though the whole thing was, as I say, like the duels of archangels) I saw suddenly what I was doing.

Actually, of course, Hopkins did "produce": there is a substantial body of verse, a surprising preponderance of which—surprising, when we consider his situation and the difficulties in the way of success—deserves currency among the classics of the language. His supreme triumphs, unquestionably classical achievements, are the last sonnets—the "terrible sonnets" together with *Justus es,* the one just quoted, and that inscribed *To R.B.* (who prints it with the unsanctioned and deplorable substitution of "moulds" for "combs" in the sixth line). These, in their achieved "smoother style," triumphantly justify the oddest extravagances of his experimenting. Technique here is the completely unobtrusive and marvellously economical and efficient servant of the inner need, the pressure to be defined and conveyed. At the other extreme are such things as *Tom's Garland* and *Harry Ploughman,* where, in the absence of controlling pressure from within, the elaborations and ingenuities of "inscape" and of expressive license result in tangles of knots and strains that no amount of reading can reduce to satisfactory rhythm or justifiable complexity. In between come the indubitable successes of developed "inscape": *The Wreck of the Deutschland* (which seems to me a great poem—at least for the first two-thirds of it), *The Windhover, Spelt from Sibyl's Leaves,* and, at the lower level, *The Leaden Echo and the Golden Echo. Henry Purcell* calls for mention as a curious special case. There can be few readers who have not found it strangely impressive, and few who could have elucidated it without extraneous help. It is not independent of the explanatory note by Hopkins that Bridges prints; yet when one approaches it with the note fresh in mind the intended meaning seems to be sufficiently *in* the poem to allay, at any rate, the dissatisfaction caused by baffled understanding.

About Hopkins as a direct influence there seems little to say. The use of him by Left poets in the 'thirties was not of a kind to demand serious critical attention. Where he is, beyond question, to be felt is in the heightened sense, characterizing taste and criticism in our time, for what may be called the Shakespearian (as opposed to the Miltonic) potentialities of English.

BIBLIOGRAPHY

I. GERARD MANLEY HOPKINS

The date and place are those of first publication. The publisher of Hopkins' work, whether in poetry or in prose, is the Oxford University Press.

Poems, edited with notes by Robert Bridges, critical introduction by Charles Williams. London, 1930.

The Letters of Gerard Manley Hopkins to Robert Bridges, edited with notes and an introduction by Claude Colleer Abbott. London, 1935.

The Correspondence of Gerard Manley Hopkins and Richard Watson Dixon, edited with notes and an introduction by Claude Colleer Abbott. London, 1935.

The Notebooks and Papers of Gerard Manley Hopkins, edited with notes and a preface by Humphry House. London, 1937.

Further Letters of Gerard Manley Hopkins: including his Correspondence with Coventry Patmore, edited with notes and an introduction by Claude Colleer Abbott. London, 1938.

Selections from the Note-Books of Gerard Manley Hopkins, edited by T. Weiss. New Directions, New York, 1945.

II. SECONDARY STUDIES

1. Biography

Bridges, Robert, *Three Friends: Memoirs of Digby Mackwork Dolben, Richard Watson Dixon, Henry Bradley*, London, 1932.

D'Arcy, Martin C., "Hopkins," in *Great Catholics*, edited by Claude Williamson, London, 1939.

Lahey, Gerald F., S.J., *Gerard Manley Hopkins*, London, 1930.

Ruggles, Eleanor, *Gerard Manley Hopkins: A Life*, New York, 1944.

2. Exegesis and Appraisal

Bremond, André, "La Poésie Naïve et Savante de Gerard Hopkins," *Etudes, Revue Catholique d'Intérêt Général*, 1934, pp. 23–49.

Croce, Benedetto, "Un gesuita inglese poeta: G. M. Hopkins," *La Critica*, xxxv, 1937, pp. 81–100.

Downey, Harris, "Hopkins: A Study in Influences," *Southern Review*, I, 1936, pp. 837–845.

Fletcher, John Gould, "Hopkins—Priest or Poet?" *American Review*, VI, 1936, pp. 331–346.

Gardner, W. H., "The Wreck of the Deutschland," Essays and Studies by Members of the English Association, XXI, 1936.

——— "A Note on Hopkins and Duns Scotus," *Scrutiny*, V, 1936, pp. 61–70.

——— "The Religious Problem in Hopkins," *Scrutiny*, VI, 1937, pp. 32–42.

——— G. M. Hopkins: *A Study of Poetic Idiosyncrasy in Relation to Poetic Tradition*, Vol. I, London, 1944.

Grisewood, H., "Gerard Manley Hopkins, S.J.," *Dublin Review*, CLXXXIX, 1931, pp. 213–226.

Heywood, Terrence, "Hopkins' Ancestry," *Poetry*, LIV, 1939, pp. 271–279.

Kelly, Bernard, *The Mind of Gerard Manley Hopkins*, Ditchling, Sussex, 1935.

Leavis, F. R., "Gerard Manley Hopkins," *New Bearings in English Poetry*, London, 1932.

Lilly, Gweneth, *"The Welsh Influence in the Poetry of Hopkins,"* Modern Language Review, XXXVIII, 1935, pp. 192–205.

Page, Frederick, "Father Gerard Hopkins: His Poetry," *Dublin Review*, 167, 1920, pp. 40–66.

Phare, Elsie Elizabeth, *"The Poetry of G. M. Hopkins: A Survey and Commentary*, Cambridge, 1933.

Pick, John, *G. M. Hopkins: Priest and Poet*, London, 1942.

BIBLIOGRAPHY

Read, Herbert, "Gerard Manley Hopkins," *In Defense of Shelley and Other Essays*, London, 1936.

Richards, I. A., "The Windhover," *Dial*, VIII, 1926, pp. 195–203.

Sargent, Daniel, "Hopkins," *Four Independents*, New York, 1935.

Sitwell, Edith, "Hopkins," *Aspects of Modern Poetry*, London, 1934.

Waterhouse, John F., "Gerard Manley Hopkins and Music," *Music and Letters*, XVIII, 1937, pp. 227–235.

Weiss, T., "G. M. Hopkins: Realist on Parnassus," *Accent*, V, 1945, pp. 135–144.

INDEX

139

INDEX

141

INDEX

143